Using Flash in Dreamweaver

p. 82

"One of the benefits of using Dreamweaver for web development is that it offers you limitless possibilities for integrating and managing Flash content on web pages."

—Edoardo Zubler

...ng Ad System in ASP.NET

p. 116

"When I was given this assignment, I wanted to be able to show everyone how amazing ASP.NET is."

—Joel Martinez

Sending a Form to Email

p. 92

"Since email communication was on my mind, Massimo and I turned quickly to talking about a common use of email in web development: a form is submitted, and an email is spit out."

—Danilo Celic, Jr.

Creating Dynamic Navigation with Server.Execute

p. 126

"I finally switched to using Server.Execute to load my calendar and was able to work on it completely independent from the rest of my blog. I became a Server.Execute convert."

—Daniel Short

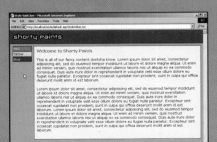

Setting Styles Dynamically

p. 104

"…led me to discover the wonders of CSS and how you can use them to change every facet of a site by swapping out a single file."

—Daniel Short

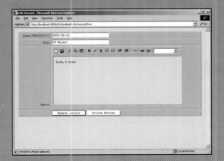

Producing a Sophisticated Interface for CMS with ColdFusion

p. 136

"So to that end, we give you the ColdFusion XHTML Editor. No more messy client code to deal with."

—Angela C. Buraglia, Massimo Foti, and Daniel Short

The photograph of the mask on the cover of this book was taken during the Fasnacht, a carnival held in Basel, Switzerland. The festival is rooted in local German/Swiss tradition, and is well-known for its party atmosphere, colorful carnival cos-tumes, and Guggen music played by the brass bands. Author Massimo Foti currently lives in Switzerland; the country is also the homeland of author Edoardo Zubler.

Macromedia®

Dreamweaver® MX 2004 Magic

Massimo Foti, Angela C. Buraglia, and Daniel Short
with Kim Cavanaugh, Danilo Celic, Kevin French, Brad Halstead, Joel Martinez, Stephanie Sullivan, Murray R. Summers, and Edoardo Zubler

New Riders

800 East 96th Street, 3rd Floor, Indianapolis, Indiana 46240
An Imprint of Pearson Education
Boston • Indianapolis • London • Munich • New York • San Francisco

Contents at a Glance

Macromedia® Dreamweaver MX® 2004 Magic

International Standard Book Number: 0-7357-1378-2

Library of Congress Catalog Card Number: 2003112374

Printed in the United States of America

First printing: December, 2003

08 07 06 05 04 03   7 6 5 4 3 2 1

Interpretation of the printing code: The rightmost double-digit number is the year of the book's printing; the rightmost single-digit number is the number of the book's printing. For example, the printing code 03-1 shows that the first printing of the book occurred in 2003.

Trademarks

All terms mentioned in this book that are known to be trademarks or service marks have been appropriately capitalized. New Riders Publishing cannot attest to the accuracy of this information. Use of a term in this book should not be regarded as affecting the validity of any trademark or service mark. Dreamweaver is a registered trademark of Macromedia.

Warning and Disclaimer

Every effort has been made to make this book as complete and as accurate as possible, but no warranty of fitness is implied. The information is provided on an as-is basis. The authors and New Riders Publishing shall have neither liability nor responsibility to any person or entity with respect to any loss or damages arising from the information contained in this book or from the use of the CD or programs that may accompany it.

Publisher
Stephanie Wall

Production Manager
Gina Kanouse

Senior Acquisitions Editor
Linda Bump Harrison

Development Editors
Linda Laflamme
Lisa Thibault

Project Editor
Michael Thurston

Indexer
Angie Bess

Proofreader
Debbie Williams

Composition
Kim Scott

Manufacturing Coordinator
Dan Uhrig

Interior Designer
Alan Clements

Cover Designer
Aren Howell

Media Developer
Jay Payne

Marketing
Scott Cowlin
Tammy Detrich
Hannah Onstad Latham

Publicity Manager
Susan Nixon

Let Us Hear Your Voice

As the reader of this book, you are the most important critic and commentator. We value your opinion and want to know what we're doing right, what we could do better, what areas you'd like to see us publish in, and any other words of wisdom you're willing to pass our way.

As the Senior Acquisitions Editor for New Riders Publishing, I welcome your comments. You can fax, email, or write me directly to let me know what you did or didn't like about this book—as well as what we can do to make our books stronger. When you write, please be sure to include this book's title, ISBN, and author, as well as your name and phone or fax number. I will carefully review your comments and share them with the author and editors who worked on the book.

Please note that I cannot help you with technical problems related to the topic of this book, and that due to the high volume of email I receive, I might not be able to reply to every message.

Fax: 317-428-3280

Email: linda.bump@newriders.com

Mail: Linda Bump Harrison
          Senior Acquisitions Editor
          New Riders Publishing
          800 East 96th Street, 3rd Floor
          Indianapolis, IN 46240 USA

About the Authors

Massimo Foti

Massimo began using Dreamweaver on the very day the first beta was available, and he has used Dreamweaver ever since.

Massimo has been a prolific extension developer since the pioneering days of Dreamweaver 1. He is the creator of www.massimocorner.com, and winner of the Macromedia Best Extension Developer award in 2000 and Top New Extension for Dreamweaver MX. His extensions are featured on the Macromedia Exchange for Dreamweaver and have been featured in many books and magazines.

He is a certified Dreamweaver developer and certified Advanced ColdFusion developer. His tips, articles and custom tags for ColdFusion are available on www.cfmentor.com, the web site of the Italian CFUG.

Massimo works at www.amila.ch developing database driven websites using ColdFusion and PHP with different RDMSs, his work ranges from database design to server- and client-side programming for web-based applications.

An avid reader of computer books, he often works as tech editor, contributor, and reviewer for publishers like Osborne, New Riders, Glasshaus, and O'Reilly.

Acknowledgment: Thanks to Angela and Dan for brilliantly taking care of all the dirty jobs, allowing me to just have fun with code. To all the people at www.amila.ch; most of my work on this book is inspired by what we do there day by day. As you may know, ColdFusion developers get the best women (even if Macromedia doesn't tell you about that); so once again I had the pleasure to work with the wonderful ladies at New Riders. Very special thanks to Federica and Tiziana, for all the times I sit in front of a PC and forget about the rest. You are the best things in my life.

Angela C. Buraglia

Angela used to be a makeup artist for independent film, but she needed a career that would allow her to work from home and raise her son. Although she intended only to be a web developer, life's path has led her to become that and more. She is perhaps best known as the founder of DreamweaverFAQ.com, a site dedicated to serving the Dreamweaver community which she continues to run today with Daniel Short. In addition to this book, Angela is also the co-author of *Dreamweaver MX Killer Tips* and *Dreamweaver MX 2004 Killer Tips* with Joseph Lowery. She was a contributing author to *Dreamweaver MX Magic*, the lead technical editor for the *Dreamweaver MX Bible* (Wiley), and a contributing author to *ColdFusion MX Web Application Construction Kit* (Macromedia Press). Long gone are the days of applying makeup; now Angela applies Behaviors and CSS to web sites—and most importantly—is home with her little boy.

Acknowledgment: Massimo, your guidance since I started Dreamweaver is really worth more than mere thanks. I'm not sure I could ever repay you (but keep reading). Daniel Short, this book just wouldn't be the same without your magic touch. Working with my best friend is always a pleasure. I couldn't have done this book without your help and support. Next time I see you two, count on dinner. I would be remiss to not mention all the people who have helped and inspired me throughout the years, unfortunately I can't name all of you in this small space. I am forever thankful to you nonetheless. Linda Bump, I've learned so much about the authoring process from you and I appreciate all you've done for me. Thanks to the team at New Riders. I must say that this has been one incredible group of people to work with; thank you to all of the contributing authors.

About the Authors

Daniel Short

Dan is the chief developer for Web Shorts Site Design as well as a devoted Team Macromedia Volunteer and uses almost the entire Macromedia Studio including Fireworks, ColdFusion, and Dreamweaver. He helps to maintain several HTML and Dreaweaver reference sites including www.dwfaq.com, for which he created the style changer and all ASP functionality, including the Snippets Exchange and the DWfaq Store.

He's also written articles for several resource sites, including AListApart.com, Spider-Food.net, the MM Designer and Developer Center (www.macromedia.com/desdev) and DWfaq.com. Dan is also a contributing author for the dynamic chapters in the *Dreamweaver MX Bible* (Wiley) and the previous edition of *Dreamweaver MX Magic*. He has also presented at several Dreamweaver conferences including the first two TODCONs and CFNorth.

Acknowledgment: I'd like to thank all of the wonderful people in this industry who have allowed me to stand on their shoulders so I could reach a little higher. I wouldn't be where I am today without the likes of Massimo (yes, even though you harass me about ColdFusion) and Angela helping me out day to day, whether through helping me learn or simply bombarding me with feature requests. And a special thanks to the Lindas, for keeping us artsy types in line and making sure that we produced the best material we could.

Kim Cavanaugh

Kim is a teacher for the School District of Palm Beach County (Florida) where he has been teaching middle school students web design using Dreamweaver, Fireworks, and Flash since 1999. Kim is also an adjunct professor at Palm Beach Community College where he teaches Dreamweaver and Flash.

The author of two beginner's guides for Dreamweaver and Fireworks (Osborne/McGraw-Hill), Kim has also developed course materials for the Learning Library (UK) and contributed to the *Macromedia Studio MX Bible* (Wiley). Kim has contributed numerous articles to Macromedia DevNet and writes extensively for CommunityMX.com, covering the full range of Studio MX products.

Kim lives in West Palm Beach with his wife and daughter and loves all things associated with life in South Florida—especially warm weather, the Miami Dolphins, inshore fishing, and Jimmy Buffett tunes.

Acknowledgment: As always, my thanks to the beautiful brown-eyed girls in my life, Kayleen and Katy, for your love, support, and patience.

About the Authors

Danilo Celic, Jr.

Every journey starts with an itch that needs to be scratched. For Danilo, the itch was a two years' out-of-date company phone book. Because of that phone book, Danilo decided to take matters into his own hands, learning HTML via the hand code in Notepad-save-preview in browser-rinse/lather/repeat method of creating web pages. First introduced to Dreamweaver at version 1.2 from a cover CD off an imported computer magazine, Danilo soon learned that coding everything manually wasn't all it was cracked up to be, and jumped in using every version since. Currently a partner at CommunityMX.com and a member of Team Macromedia, Danilo frequently comes to the aid of budding extension developers in the Macromedia support forums. While the languages of the web world change continuously, the late hours stay the same, which is unfortunate for his lovely wife, Melissa.

Acknowledgment: Thanks to my wife, Melissa, for her unceasing patience when I spend way too much time on computer stuff. Also, thanks to Angela Buraglia for being so kind and wonderful, and mostly for never giving up when I say it can't be done. To Dan Short, for server space and not laughing too hard at my bad jokes. To Massimo, for his generosity in sharing his expertise in many topics, from coding to water polo coaching. And to the three of them for asking me to participate in this wonderful little project.

Kevin French

Kevin is the founder and president of MM2K Inc., a full service Internet company. Formed in 1998 as simply a web design agency, MM2K has expanded its suite of services to also include Internet access, web hosting, dynamic application development, custom e-commerce solutions, and strategic Internet consulting. On the design and development front, Kevin is a self-taught Fireworks designer and a Macromedia Dreamweaver Developer Certified Professional. His design, development, and project management skills have earned him and his company numerous industry awards and accolades. His clientele list includes United States Governors, Senators, Congressman, professional athletes, state universities, and established corporations.

Kevin has been a lifetime resident of the beautiful New Jersey shore. When he is not "plugged in," you can find him mountain biking, hiking, and driving on the back country roads of New Jersey.

Acknowledgment: I would like to thank my beautiful girlfriend, Jocelyn, for supporting and motivating me to help me achieve my dreams. Together, the world and ultimate happiness is ours. I love you. I would like to thank Mark Haynes of Macromedia for sharing his vast knowledge of Fireworks since I began using it when it was first introduced. Mark is a true asset to Macromedia and the entire Macromedia community. Kleanthis Economou (www.projectfireworks.com) and Linda Rathberger (www.playingwithfire.com) have both been instrumental in my understanding of Fireworks and I am grateful for their assistance through the years.

About the Authors

Brad Halstead

Brad (www.dreamweavermx-templates.com) is a computer software engineering technologist by trade, but deviated from that dream to join the Canadian military as an air weapons systems technician where he learned all about various computerized aircraft weapons systems as well as loading the munitions. Brad has dabbled in the web in various capacities since 1989 and left the military to become a full-time computer technician. Brad tries to play an active roll in the support forums for Dreamweaver, Contribute and Project Seven, as time permits him to. Brad is HTML 4.01 Certified, and has contributed content to *Dreamweaver MX Magic* and *Inside Dreamweaver MX*, in addition to being a technical editor for both publications. Recently, Brad co-authored *Dreamweaver MX Templates* and has been accepted as a Team Macromedia Member for Contribute.

He lives in London, Ontario with his cherished partner Brenda and their daughters Megan and Amanda, son Aaron, two Yorkshire Terriers, and their newest addition, a Sheltie.

Acknowledgment: Thank you to the following people for inviting me to participate in this project: Massimo Foti, Angela Buraglia, Dan Short, and Linda Bump. I'd like to also thank Linda Laflamme (Copy Editor), the Tech Editors (Danilo Celic and Matt Brown), and all the other people involved in the book's production. Of course, thanks to Macromedia for engineering Dreamweaver MX 2004!

Joel Martinez

Joel creates enterprise-level web applications using the .NET Framework (amongst other technologies). He started the Orlando .NET User Group to promote the use of .NET within his local community and strives to teach anyone who will listen the virtues of Microsoft's brainchild. He is also a partner at Community MX (www.communitymx.com).

Acknowledgment: First and foremost I'd like to thank God for giving me the opportunity to work on such a wonderful project. Thanks to the New Riders team for allowing me to spread the .NET gospel. Much thanks goes out to my high school teacher, Sharon Christensen-Jones; she is a testament to the important role teachers play in our society. To my parents for always working hard to give me what I needed, and my brother for always lending a hand. Last, but certainly not least, I'd like to thank my wife and daughter, Tabbitha and Layla, for being so supportive in this and other ventures. I love you.

About the Authors

Stephanie Sullivan

Stephanie is a web developer, a partner at CommunityMX (www.communitymx.com), and owner of VioletSky Design (www.violetsky.net). Somewhere in all that, she is also the wife of a screenwriter and mother of two awesome boys who she has home schooled all their lives.

In addition to her articles at Macromedia's DevNet Center, her weekly writing and support at CommunityMX focuses on Dreamweaver, design principles, CSS, HTML/XHTML, color, and web business issues. Stephanie's background in art and color theory as well as her deep interest in standards, CSS, and accessibility, allow her to create highly visual, standards-compliant, low-bandwidth web sites.

In her spare time, of which there is sadly very little, she spends time with her family at the beach, the historic downtown district, and geocaching with her boys. To force herself "out of the chair" she recently joined a volleyball team.

Acknowledgment: I am deeply indebted to those who have paved the way for the standards revolution—Jeffrey Zeldman and Eric Meyer are my two favorites, as much for their humor as their brilliance and bravery. Also, much thanks goes to my favorite bug squashers and friends: "Big John" Gallant, Holly Bergevin, and Philippe Whittenberg who have helped me work out numerous browser issues over the past few months. To my husband Timothy, thanks for your support, guidance, love, and patience. I know it hasn't been easy. And to my sons Cameron and Hunter, I know it's tough at times when mom "goes missing." Thanks for filling in the gaps around the house. You guys are the best. I love you.

Murray R. Summers

Although a biochemist by training, Murray has spent the last 20 years working in the computer industry. In 1998, Murray started his own web site production company, Great Web Sights (www.great-web-sights.com). As a Team Macromedia member, he also participates in the sponsored forums for Dreamweaver and other products. He lives in rural Philadelphia with his lovely wife Suzanne, their teenaged daughter Carly, a Golden Retriever, an Eskipoo, a mutt of unknown derivation, and a goldfish.

Murray is a Macromedia Certified Web Site Developer and Dreamweaver Developer, and has contributed chapters to *Dreamweaver 4 Magic* by Al Sparber, and *Dreamweaver 4: The Missing Manual*, by David Sawyer McFarland (Pogue Press/O'Reilly). He has authored the premier treatment of advanced Template properties, *Dreamweaver MX Templates* with Brad Halstead. He has managed to embarrass himself several times as an invited speaker at TODCON, TODCON II, TODCON North, and TODCON MX.

Acknowledgment: Thank you to Al Sparber for his generous teaching on the Macromedia Dreamweaver Forum. Thank you also to David McFarland for teaching me the technique of using Optional Regions in his excellent *Dreamweaver MX: The Missing Manual* (Pogue Press/O'Reilly).

About the Authors

Edoardo Zubler

Edoardo is a multimedia developer who specializes in creating rich media applications for a wide range of devices and platforms. He has produced both front end and back end solutions for tablet PCs, set-top boxes, and handheld PDAs. During his career he has been involved in pioneering projects such as the development and implementation of a content repurposing system based on Macromedia Generator for the first regular digital terrestrial (DVB-t) data broadcasting service in Europe. He has developed many Flash-based rich client applications for fixed and mobile devices.

As a Team Macromedia Volunteer, Edoardo has written several articles and developed a number extensions for many Macromedia products including FlashBang! (www.flashbangmedia.com) with Joseph Lowery. He also runs Aftershape (www.aftershape.com), his own personal web site, where he showcases his "digital oddities".

Acknowledgment: I'd like to thank my family for all the support. Many thanks to the authors of this book and the people at New Riders for their friendliness. A special thank-you to Massimo Foti for all the help he has given me and for being such a good friend.

About the Technical Reviewers

Developing technically accurate books is a priority at New Riders. We rely on the skills and advice of technical experts to guide the authors in the creation and development of their manuscripts. The following reviewers have provided their input—and we offer our thanks for their hard work and dedication.

Matt Brown

Matt is a consultant based in the San Francisco Bay Area. He has edited more than 20 Dreamweaver and Photoshop books over the years. He has taught at Foothill College and the Multimedia Studies Program at San Francisco State University. He was on the Dreamweaver team for five years in a number of capacities, and finally as Community Manager. Matt is married to a magnificent woman, Marcella, and he keeps chickens, loves to cook, and creates all sorts of art.

Danilo Celic, Jr.

Danilo learned HTML via the hand code in Notepad-save-preview in browser-rinse/lather/repeat method of creating web pages. First introduced to Dreamweaver at version 1.2 from a cover CD off an imported computer magazine, Danilo soon learned that coding everything manually wasn't all it was cracked up to be, and jumped in using every version since. Currently a partner at CommunityMX.com and a member of Team Macromedia, Danilo frequently comes to the aid of budding extension developers in the Macromedia support forums.

Table of Contents

Table of Conents

Table of Contents

How to Make the Most of This Book

This book has been created with special elements in order to make your experience with the manuscript more productive.

- Each project opens with a statement from the author explaining why he or she chose this particular technique or project to share with you and how it will help you in your work. You'll also get a quick, illustrated overview of the project in the section called "It Works Like This."

- Before you start diving into each project, there are several tasks you need to complete in order to prepare your workspace and files. This is covered in the "Preparing to Work" sections.

- At the end of each project, a section called "Now Try This" suggests other ways to apply the methods you've learned, or ways to adapt the project you've just completed, whether it's building on the project itself or swapping out some functionality.

- In addition to the code listings and exercise files on the accompanying CD-ROM, you'll find videos that clearly demonstrate step by step all the procedures you need to complete in order to create the projects.

Conventions Used in This Book

As you work through the projects, keep in mind the following conventions we've used:

- Project files and folders provided on the accompanying CD appear in the text like this: **bold**.

- Many of the techniques in this book require adding or altering some code. All code is highlighted and identified in the text with a listing number (such as Listing 2.3). To apply the code, you can either enter it yourself or locate the listing on the CD, then copy and paste it into your project. To copy the code for a project from the CD, go to that project's **Code listings** folder and open the corresponding listing text file. For example, the code file for Listing 2.3 is identified on the CD as **listing02–03.txt**.

- The ➡ symbol appearing in code indicates that the line of code continues on the next line. If you are entering that code by hand, you should simply type it in as one line, without the continuation symbol.

- Text you are asked to enter into fields or code listings will appear like this: underscored.

- Text that appears inside code listings will appear in a special font, like this: code.

- Commands and keyboard shortcuts for both Windows and Mac are included throughout the projects. The Windows option is listed first, then its Mac equivalent, like this: Ctrl/Cmd+B, which means "Hold down the Control key on Windows and press the B key, or on the Mac, press Command and B."

Enjoy creating the magic!
—The New Riders Staff

Using CSS to Position and Style Your Pages

Stephanie Sullivan

Stephanie Sullivan writes regularly for Community MX, and has written for Macromedia's DevNet Center and MX Developer's Journal on topics like Dreamweaver, CSS, XHTML, and color and design principles. She is owner of VioletSky Design.

Though writing code initially attracted me to web design, I was immediately entranced by graphics, color, and imagery. I'm a strong believer in the psychological effects of color and images, and the enhanced marketing ability they offer when used properly. Then I learned about download time, the great equalizer. Oh dear. Luckily, it wasn't too long before I learned about CSS. The possibilities began to look promising.

CSS fascinated me and I began by using it to style text. Then I moved on to background colors and buttons. The control it gives and the time it saves is awesome. Little by little I used more CSS and less graphics in my designs until one day I realized my web pages were becoming a bit boring. That's when I began experimenting with new ways of creating less boxy looks using CSS. You really can have your cake and eat it too! Quick downloading pages that are still attractive are within the realm of possibility using CSS. We've only just begun with this!

It Works Like This

Because this project relies entirely on CSS for styling and positioning, you can customize it in countless ways. This is a truly simple way to create a three-column layout. Depending on your current expertise in the CSS realm, you may choose to follow the project exactly or you may want to tweak it as you go. Here are the basic steps of the project:

1   Learn a method of *Tromp l'oeil* (a French term meaning "to fool the eye") that makes the viewer believe they are seeing through certain elements on your page using a fixed background image applied to various page elements.

2   Learn to use the CSS cascade to really take control of your page. Use fonts creatively to replace images.

3   Learn to style elements that are next to each other in the flow of the document using adjacent sibling selectors.

4   Show a different button style to indicate which page the user is on, without any server-side code or JavaScript—only CSS.

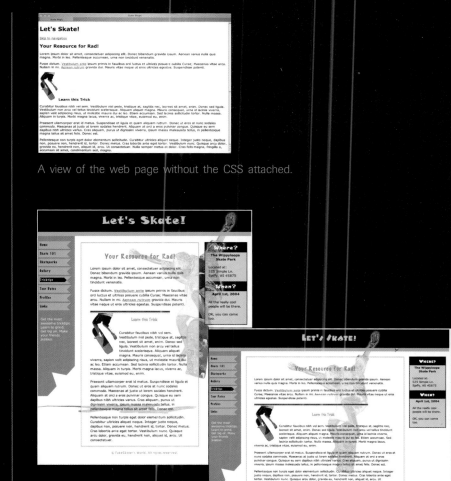

A view of the web page without the CSS attached.

The completed project viewed at two different screen resolutions.

Preparing to Work

To prepare for this project, you will need to do the following:

1   Copy the **Projects/01** folder from the CD to your hard drive.

2   Define a new site using the **01** copy as your site root.

3   Take a look at the files that came with the project as well as the markup inside them. Rather than have you type in a lot of filler text, I've provided the XHTML document called **index.htm**. In addition to the extension you just installed, the **01** folder contains **index.htm**, **indexfinal.htm**, **skater.css**, and an **assets** folder which contains images.

    The **skater.css** file is the completed CSS document that you may want to use for reference. It styles the indexfinal.htm document. The CSS Snippets will be used as code snippets throughout the project. You will need to download Andrew Clover's **fixed.js** document. It is already linked in the head of both index.htm and indexfinal.htm. Due to a bug in IE6, you won't be able to view the project properly without it in that browser (www.dwmagic.com/go/13).

4   Open the **Extensions** folder and install the extension **Project 01 Snippets.mxp**. See Appendix A, "Installing Extensions," for instructions.

5   Open the **index.htm** file and look at each section of the document so that you'll be familiar with what you've got and where you're going.

6   Preview the index page in a browser and notice the structure of the page. Although the page is unstyled and plain, all information is available and easy to access.

The page begins with an XHTML Transitional doctype. This comprises the first two lines of the document and comes before the `<html>` tag. Nothing should come before the doctype (including the XML Prologue) or you will put IE6 into quirks mode. *Quirks mode* means it will render your page according to older, less standard methods. (See www.dwmagic.com/go/14 to learn more about doctypes and quirks mode.)

7   Familiarize yourself with the structure of the document by viewing this page in Dreamweaver's Code view.

8   If you'd like to view the final project before you get started, open the **indexfinal.htm** document in your browser either from your local drive or upload it to your web site (along with the associated images, fixed.js, and CSS file) and view it there. Increase the text size using the controls in your specific browser and make the browser window different sizes to view the effect.

Browser Compatibility

This project has been tested for functionality in the following browsers:

- Microsoft Internet Explorer 5.0, 5.5, 6 (Windows)
- Microsoft Internet Explorer 5.2.2 (Macintosh)
- Netscape 6 and 7 (Windows and Macintosh)
- Mozilla 1.4 (Windows)
- Mozilla 1.3b (Macintosh)
- Opera 7 (Windows)
- Camino 0.7.0 (Macintosh)
- Safari 1.0 (Macintosh)

Creating the Structure for the Page

Now that you've looked at the XHTML document's syntax, you're going to begin to move the <div> tags into place. Remember that a <div> is 100% as wide as its containing element. If a <div> tag is not contained in another <div> tag or element, its parent container is <body> and <html> is the grand-parent. You can use <div>s rather like building blocks or stacked boxes to create your structure.

1   Open the index.htm document. In the CSS Styles panel, click the New CSS Style icon to open a New CSS Style dialog box. Choose Selector Type: Advanced, Define in: New Style Sheet, and type <u>html, body</u> into the Selector text box. Click the OK button of the New CSS Style dialog. Name the file <u>project1.css</u>, ensure the Relative to field is set to Document and that you are located in the root of your site in the Save Style Sheet File As dialog, and click the Save button.

You've now linked your style sheet to your index.htm document.

2   In the CSS Style definition dialog that now appears, choose the following:

Category: Box

Padding: Check Same for All and enter <u>0</u>

Margin: Check Same for All and enter <u>0</u>

Category: Border

Width: Check Same for All and enter <u>0</u>

Click OK

This is done to force all browsers to begin with zero for the page margins and borders. Browsers have different default settings, and this allows all to start on a level playing field.

Tip: Border is declared on the HTML element to get rid of the IE Windows invisible border. You'll get more consistent results if you zero it out.

Note: If you'd like to see the power of CSS through "instant styling" of your page, click the Attach Style Sheet in the CSS Styles panel and browse to the **skater.css** file. Click the Preview button, and watch the page jump to life. Obviously, you'll want to click Cancel before you close.

---

3   Click the New CSS Style icon at the bottom of the CSS Styles panel. In the dialog that appears, choose the following, then click OK:

Tag: body

Selector Type: Tag (redefines the look of a specific tag)

Define In: project1.css

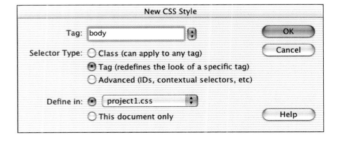

4   In the CSS Style definition dialog, choose the following:

   Category: Type

      Font: Verdana, Geneva, Arial, Helvetica, sans-serif

      Size: 100%

      Color: #000

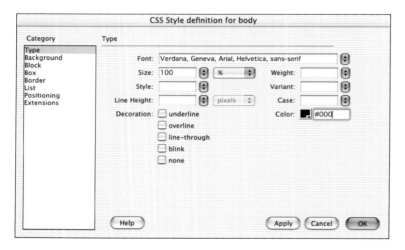

   Category: Background

      Background Color: #FFF

      Background Image: Browse to the **skater.jpg** image in
      the assets folder. (For simplicity, save your CSS and
      images relative to the document.)

      Repeat: no-repeat

      Attachment: fixed

      Horizontal Position: 0%

      Vertical Position: 0%

Tip: The color attributes in step 4 are set using color shorthand. This is a quicker way to write any color that contains hex-pairs (00, 33, 66, 99, CC, FF, and so on). It's a simple formula, really. Take the first character for each hex-pair and drop the second. For example, #000000 becomes #000, #336699 becomes #369, and #CCFFFF becomes #CFF.

5   Click the OK button to save the new style definition.

   The W3C specs say that Attachment: fixed, on the background image, aligns it to the viewport (not its containing element). You'll see why this is so important for the effect you're creating in a little while. Also, you may wonder what the font size set to 100% means. 100% of what? The users' preferences. The browser will start with whatever they've defined in their browser and then scale the sizes from there.

Tip: You should be aware of the CSS preferences: Edit > Preferences > CSS Styles. If you prefer to have your CSS files open when you're modifying a style, leave the check mark in the Open CSS Files When Modified box. You will have to save your CSS page before the styles will appear on your index.htm page. If you prefer to do your editing in the CSS Styles panel or the Relevant CSS tab of the Tag inspector, uncheck this box or your CSS document will open each time you make an edit.

You may also want to set your CSS to write in shorthand. This is another way to save page weight and is what I'll be demonstrating in the code later in this chapter.

Defining the *<div>*s

Now it's time to define the various <div>s. You'll start with the header <div>. If you haven't yet, try using the Property inspector to create a style and edit your style sheet. It's good to use each of the methods Dreamweaver offers to find what works with your personal workflow.

1   Make sure the index.htm document is the active document. Using the Property inspector, select Manage Styles from the Style select box and create a CSS Selector called <u>div#header</u>. In the Edit Style Sheet dialog, highlight project1.css and choose New. Use the following settings:

    Selector: div#header

    Selector Type: Advanced (IDs, contextual selectors, etc.)

    Define in: project1.css

Tip: Be aware of document focus when creating new CSS styles with the CSS Styles panel. If you have the project1.css document active while creating a new style, choose Define In: This Document Only. Likewise, if the index.htm document has focus, you'll want to choose Define in: project1.css.

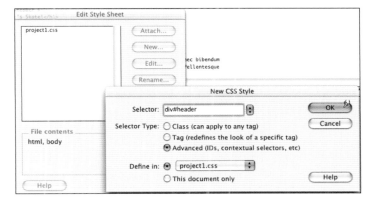

2   Apply the following code in the dialog that appears. Place these properties in the following categories: Background, Border, and Positioning.

Listing 1.1

```
div#header {
    border-bottom: 15px solid #92C837;
    position: relative;
    z-index: 1;
    height: 5em;
    background: #000 url(assets/skaterblack.jpg) 0% 0%
    ➥no-repeat fixed;
}
```

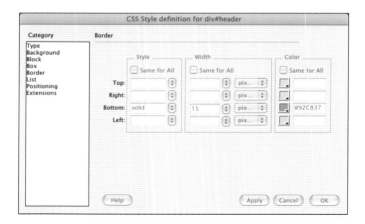

Notice that the background image of the header <div> is identical to, but the opposite colors of, the body selector? That's part of the see-through effect first invented by Eric Meyer, CSS guru extraordinaire. Make sure you give your background the same color as the image. This way if a browser area is larger than the image you've used, the background color will give it a seamless transition.

Note: The selector could have been created as #header, but div#header is more specific. It says that any <div> with the id of header should be styled as instructed. It is a safer and more specific way to style.

For the rest of this project, I'll give you the name of the CSS code snippet to use for that step. You can either define your selectors using the CSS Style panel, Property inspector, insert the snippet into a blank CSS document, and paste them into your project1.css or insert the snippet directly into your project1.css (due to the order you'll add in some of the declarations, you may want to paste the selectors from one document to the other to keep them in a logical order).

The position: relative is given to the header <div> because you cannot define a z-index (stacking order) in a <div> without a position defined. (I'll discuss the reasons for the z-index in this page further along in the project.) It doesn't adversely affect the flow of the page, however.

3 Style the navigational <div>. Unless you choose to create these styles by hand, in your Snippets panel, go to the **MX Magic 2004 > Project 01** folder. Highlight the **01-DIV CSS** snippet and with your cursor at the bottom of the projects1.css document, click Insert. Notice that you've just added three new selectors (more on these later).

4 Save project1.css and view the index.htm page in Dreamweaver's Design view, as well as in your favorite standards-compliant browser.

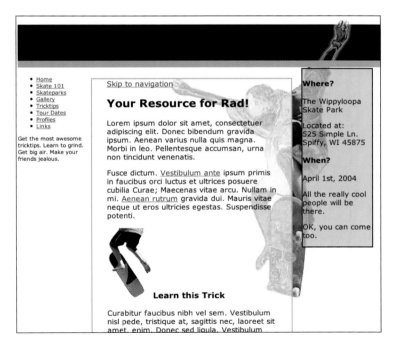

Notice how the page is beginning to take shape. You styled the left navigational <div> (div#nav) and absolutely positioned it. It is taken out of the flow of the document, and it will stay in the space you just defined. It won't be affected by the other elements in the flow of the page. It will always start 6em from the top and be right at the left browser chrome.

You defined all sizing of this <div> in relative units (em). If a user has any visual difficulty and bumps the browser's text size up, the whole page will resize relative to the new base text size (remember that you set the font size in the body to 100% of whatever the user's browser preferences are). This provides a great deal of flexibility for the end user, which is always the goal.

Note: *Margin* is the space defined on the outside of the box or <div>. *Padding* is the space defined on the inside of the box or <div>. There are some browser quirks with IE you may need to work around with certain types of designs. For more information, read "The Box Model Problem" by Holly Bergevin (www.dwmagic.com/go/15).

The padding at the top of the <div> was added due to differences in browser placement. I wanted to make sure the left nav <div> met up with the banner above it visually. I moved the top of the <div> up on the page and then added the padding and a z-index (with a lower value than the header <div>'s z-index) to allow it to meet with or go under the header <div>. The padding keeps the buttons (unordered list) aligned with the content <div> where I want them. The padding at the bottom was created to give some length to the nav <div> for the image you'll add later. It's all preference and set with my eye really, so you can have a lot of fun personalizing the styling later.

5 Look at the styling of the info <div>, which has become the right column on your page.

Once again you've created an absolutely positioned `<div>`. This time you've positioned it using top and right positioning. I made sure to keep it away from the right browser chrome because of a bug in IE5 Mac that causes a horizontal scroll bar. If you don't care about that, you can place the column right up to the edge.

Note: Once again you've used a background image fixed to the background of the browser window. This gives you yet one more image that will appear to show through its element.

---

6   For the content and footer `<div>`s, look at the selectors called `div#content` and `div#footer` that were added by the 01-DIV CSS snippet.

You'll recall you styled one absolutely positioned `<div>` relative to the left side of the document and the other absolutely positioned `<div>` relative to the right side of the document. Both of them have specific widths. This leaves the center of the page for the content `<div>` to be molded into. I've used margins to snug the content `<div>` into that space. The margins are made large enough to bypass the two outer `<div>`s. So although the content `<div>` is actually still going all the way across the page, the margins are large enough to clear the sides.

Notice that the footer `<div>` has no positioning declarations. This will allow it to flow right beneath the element it follows in the document structure—in this case, the content `<div>`.

Note: There is a fixed background for the content `<div>` as well. I wanted to make a point with this project about the variety of ways fixed backgrounds could be applied. It is only necessary to use two ways to get this effect. Depending on the file sizes, it might not even be desirable to use more, so pay attention to those.

CAUTION

Be aware that Dreamweaver will not render the background `position: fixed` properly. It renders it in relation to the element. Your page will not look the same in a browser, so use Preview in Browser (F12) to see the effect.

Note: When using button-styled navigational lists, it's not important to use text links at the bottom of the page as is recommended when your navigation is images. To adaptive technology, the button-styled navigational lists appear to be fully accessible text links.

---

7   Save your work.

Creating Buttons and Background Shapes

Now that you have a grip on CSS selectors, you'll create some interesting button-styled navigation using a couple of small background images and an unordered list. You'll also take away the square look that the bottom of the navigation `<div>` would normally have. You already have the actual nav `<div>` on the page, but it doesn't yet have any background color or styling. You'll add the `<ul>`, `<li>`, `<a>`, and `<p>` styling. Each one carves out a specific area for itself that contributes to the overall style of the button area.

1   Place your cursor in the bottom of the project1.css document. In the Snippets panel, select the **MX Magic 2004 > Project 01 > 02-Button CSS** snippet and insert it into your page.

The `div#nav ul` selector adds margins on each side of the list. This keeps the space around the list so that the colored background will show when the list is styled.

Note: To be accurate and specific, all the selectors for the navigation `<div>` begin with `div#nav` and a space, and then you continue down the cascade naming each element in the document tree until you get to the name of the element you're styling. These are known as Descendant Selectors. You are defining rules for elements based on the element appearing inside of a specific `<div>` and even inside other specific elements.

The `div#nav li` selector removes the list style (bullet) and adds padding inside the `<li>` itself on the top and bottom. This begins to create a more button-like look.

`div#nav li a` is the selector that defines the actual link itself. The link must be set to `display: block` with a width of 100% to be "clickable" through the whole button area, not just on the text itself. A left margin is set to hold the text away from the left edge.

Notice the grouping of the `div#nav li a:hover, div#nav li a:focus` selectors. They are written with a comma between the selectors because they have identical declarations. The `a:focus` selector applies to the look you see when tabbing through the page. This is a good habit to get into to make your page visually more accessible.

CAUTION

Make sure when separating selectors with commas that you use the entire selector each time. For example: Due to the lack of specificity, `div#nav li a:hover, a:focus` is *not* the same as `div#nav li a:hover, div#nav li a:focus`.

2 Save your document, and preview the index file in your browser.

3 You need to add some background color and images for styling. For example, adding a white background shape (image) to the bottom of the `div#nav` will get rid of the squareness normally there. In the CSS Styles panel, highlight the selector called `div#nav`. Click the Edit icon at the bottom.

4 Go to the Background category, browse to the image called **corner.gif** in your assets folder, and set:

   Background: #897EA6

   Repeat: no-repeat

   Horizontal Position: 100%

   Vertical Position: 100%

5 Click OK. Save the CSS, and preview your page.

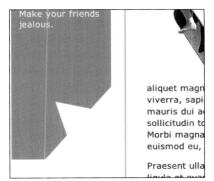

Notice the change in the navigation <div>, especially the bottom-right corner. Yes, it is still square, but it no longer appears that way visually. This background image does not have fixed positioning, so it is rendered in relation to the element it's in, not the viewport. Because the rendering is measured from the top-left corner, this graphic is set to 100% (from left), 100% (from top). This places it in the bottom-right corner.

Tip: Using this method, you can create just about anything your mind can conceive. Just make sure the image is the same color as the page background it will be placed over. Matte it with the background color of the <div> it will be sitting on, and export it as a transparent .gif for best results. This gives the illusion of a cutout area in the normally square-cornered <div>.

6   Use the same method as in steps 3 and 4 to attach a background image to the buttons. Open the div#nav li selector and add these settings:

Background: #92C837

Repeat: no-repeat

Horizontal Position: 100%

Vertical Position: 50%

URL: assets/inverted.gif

7   Add these declarations to div#nav li a:hover, div#nav li a:focus:

URL: assets/tip.gif

Repeat: no-repeat

Horizontal Positioning: 100%

Vertical Positioning: 50%

Width: 80%

Background: #000

The width is set to 80% so that the <a> element doesn't go all the way to the right edge of the <li> element, and the background image of the link area shows on hover. Notice that the positioning on these background images is set horizontally to 100% (all the way to the right side), but vertically to 50%. This keeps the center point of the graphics in the center of the button. The images were created about twice the size they appear to be at a moderate text size in case the viewer's text size is set larger or increased.

Note: I created the button background look by exporting the triangular purple shape (same as the background color it's sitting on) matted in green (same as the button it's placed in). The link background look was created by exporting a green triangular shape with a black matte.

8   Save your work.

Taking Font and Link Styling to the Next Level

Time to take a closer look at fonts, links, selectors, and the cascade. Some simple tricks will add a lot of class to your styles with only a little effort on your part. First, you're going to create a new font list for the `nav#header h1` selector. When it's completed, you'll apply it to the selector.

1 Place your cursor at the bottom of the projects1.css page. Select the **03-Fonts CSS** snippet and insert it into your document. Save your CSS file.

2 In your CSS Style panel, highlight the `nav#header h1` selector and click the Edit icon. In the Type category, click the drop-down next to Font. At the bottom of the font lists, select Edit Font List.

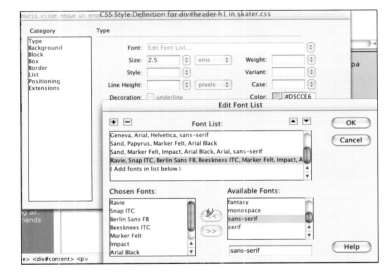

A dialog opens and gives you the ability to create an entirely new font list. I'll give you the list of fonts in the next step. Look for them, *in order*, in the Available Fonts list.

3 Select the fonts listed below from the Available Fonts list, and click the double left arrow button to add each to the Chosen Fonts list. Be sure to select and add them in the order shown:

    Ravie

    Snap ITC

    Berlin Sans FB

    Beesknees ITC

    Marker Felt

    Impact

    Arial Black

    sans-serif

If a font is not available in the Available Fonts list, type its exact name in the text box under the list and click the double left arrow button.

4 Click OK and you'll be taken back out to the CSS Style definition for the `div#header h1` selector.

Please pay close attention to the font declaration on this selector (and the ones to follow). The font cascade is a very overlooked and highly useful item. Everyone has heard of "browser-safe" fonts. And it is important to make sure some of the fonts you're using are fonts that most browsers have—but they don't all have to be. Due to the cascade order, the browser starts with the first font. If that font is found, the browser renders it on screen. If not, the browser looks for the second font, and third, and so on until it finds one of the fonts you've defined. This is the reason you should always define a generic font as the last font in your declaration. The browser will at least render serif or sans-serif.

Note: What's the logic behind the list you created? I began with Ravie, a fun, funky font that is installed with Publisher and shows up on many Windows boxes with custom installs. Then I went to Snap ITC, which is fairly similar and much more common on older (and some Mac) systems. This was followed by Berlin Sans FB and Beesknees. They are similar in look but because Beesknees appears to be more common, and I generally like the look of Berlin Sans FB more. I placed the more common one after the less common one. Marker Felt is an OS X for Macintosh font. Impact comes installed on many Windows and Mac machines. It's not my favorite, but it's better than something plain like Arial, so I added it toward the end of the cascade as a "catch-all" before Arial Black and the generic sans-serif.

Tip: Many times developers do not take advantage of this feature. There are a variety of reasons, including wanting the web to be like the print medium where things are identical—it's not—not knowing what fonts are available on the various platforms, and maybe simply not realizing the possibilities. If you take a little time one afternoon and dig around in these links, you can develop your own attractive font cascades. Code Style provides an excellent cross-platform font sampler survey with images of the fonts next to the survey results (www.dwmagic.com/go/16). Microsoft's Typography area has font listings available by product (www.dwmagic.com/go/17).

You can have headers styled with CSS instead of images. Because Windows XP now has Clear Font rendering similar to the Quartz rendering on OS X Macintosh, it won't be long before you can't tell a CSS styled header from a graphic—at least not by the ugly pixellation. This saves you download time and makes your page more accessible to all technologies.

5   Choose the font list you just created. Set the size to 2.5em. Save the CSS and view your index page.

Notice how the words in the black nav area magically seem to appear out of nowhere. This is due to the cascade order. Previously, you had not assigned a color to the h1 selector, so it was inheriting the #000 (black) from the `<body>` rule. The font was there, but because it was on a black `<div>`, it was invisible. It's now a nice light lavender for contrast. I also centered it, gave it a little letter spacing (space between each letter for legibility), and a small top margin to keep it away from the top of the browser because browsers are not consistent in their default margin and padding settings.

Note: The black text on black `<div>` issue is the reason applying a background color and font color in the same rule is the best practice. If you're sure your background below has contrast and you don't want a different background color, you can declare `background: transparent`. You'll have to add this to your style sheet by hand.

---

6   Create one more font list and apply it to the `div#nav li a` selector. Use these fonts in order:

    Kristen ITC

    Marker Felt

    Tempus Sans ITC

    Textile

    Arial Black

    Arial

    sans-serif

7   Apply the font list to the `div#nav li a` selector, select a font size of 1em, and click OK.

Note: When creating font lists, choose fonts that are similar but a mixture of what's available on different platforms and browsers for best results. For instance, the cascades I created here were funky due to the site subject/style. On a classy, feminine site, you may want to develop a nice font cascade of script-type fonts.

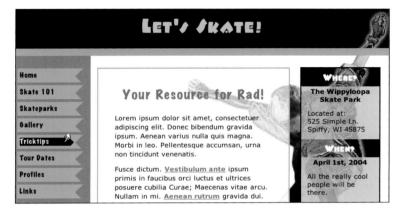

8   Look at three more of the selectors from the **03-Fonts CSS** snippet: `div#content h2`, `div#content h3`, and `div#info h4`.

There are two ways to define your fonts. Because the cascade starts at the first font and then proceeds down the list, many will use the least common, moving toward the most common. That works great if you really have no preference which font shows up on any given machine. However, if you have a definite preference (like in this project where I wanted the font to be funkified), you can also list them in the order of your most favorite, cascading down to your least favorite. Either way is effective depending on the outcome you'd like.

The remaining styles you added should be fairly self-explanatory. You should be able to discern what most of the styles are doing until you come to the `div#content p+h3` and `div#info h4+p` selectors. For more information on these selectors, please see the Adjacent Sibling Selector Styles sidebar in the next section of this project.

Notice the link styling. Nothing too fancy. You'll have to preview in a browser to see how the rollovers appear with the background color and black text. Also, make one of the links in your code actually link somewhere (maybe your own web site). Visit the linked page so that your link state, when you return to your index page, will render in the visited style. You'll see the link you just visited with a strikethrough. I think it's an easier way to spot where you've been and where you haven't, but it's a matter of preference. The point is, I didn't get rid of the underlines that some people feel are so important for usability (except on the button link styles for button-styling purposes) but still styled the links creatively.

9   Create three more selectors:

Listing 1.2

```
.fltleft{
  float: left;
}

div#skip a:link, div#skip a:visited {
  position: absolute;
  overflow: hidden;
  width: 0;
  height: 0;
}

div#skip a:active, div#skip a:focus {
  position: absolute;
  overflow: visible;
  top: 5px;
  left: 5px;
  width: auto;
  height:auto;
  background-color: #92C837;
  color: #000;
  padding: 5px;
  border: 1px solid #000;
  text-decoration: none;
  z-index: 10;
}
```

Though it is commonly believed that setting a skip link to `display:none;` allows screen readers and adaptive technology to take advantage of the link while keeping it from rendering onscreen, in many cases this is false. Some important adaptive technology will also be unable to use it, and persons who tab through web sites will also skip right over it. We're going to use a method here developed independently by Tom Gilder and Philippe Whittenberg. The trick is in setting the width and height of the div to zero and to hide the overflow. Then, in the link's active and focus states, the overflow is visible, and the width and height are set to auto and the z-index is moved up to 10. The rest of the code in these selectors is for styling purposes.

Note: Dreamweaver will not show the skip div in Design view because it will render the link state. Also, notice in Listing 1.2 that the "visited" state of the link is set the same as the "link" state. This is to keep the skip link from taking on the overall page style with a strikethrough after it has been visited.

10 Apply the `.fltleft` class to the image. In Design view, click on the image of the legs in the content `<div>`. At the bottom of the window, right-click (Ctrl-click) on img in the tag selector and select Set Class > fltleft from the Context menu.

11 Save project1.css. View the index page in a browser and notice how the `<h3>` is now next to the image—the magic of floating.

Selectors, Siblings, Descendants, and the Cascade

This next little trick came to my attention through my good friend, and IE5 Mac bug buster, Philippe Whittenberg. I'll demonstrate it using the navigation for this page. It can be even more spectacular in its style when you've got more of a "down state" button or an inline tab-styled list of

links. I call it the "you are here" trick. If you've styled CSS buttons before, you may have shown the button for the active page in its down state by changing its class or id on each page. If you use templates or Library Items, however, you have to place your navigation in an editable area in order to make those changes. This technique allows you to show a page indicator whether you use server side includes, templates, or Library Items using only the body element and CSS.

Adjacent Sibling Selector Styles

I don't have space to get deeply into sibling, descendent, or adjacent selector relationships, but the project web site has resources for you to learn more. These selectors can be very powerful. Take a look at a few examples from the project.

With the last group of snippets, we placed the div#content p+h3 and div#info h4+p selectors; these are known as *Adjacent Sibling selectors*. They allow you to take advantage of two elements that come in a specific order in your page. The first one selects any <h3> element that immediately follows a <p> element that is a descendant of a <div> element with an id attribute that equals content. (<h3> and <p> are siblings in the document tree and are selected only when they are adjacent to each other.)

This particular Adjacent Sibling selector is instructing the <h3> element, which is immediately preceded by a <p> element, to have a top border. I used a 3em line height to force the border away from the h3 header a bit.

The second selector, div#info h4+p, selects any <p> element that immediately follows an <h4> element (siblings) that is a descendant of a <div> with the id of info. In our selector, this causes the first paragraph after the <h4> element in the info div to be centered with a

bolded font. Descendant selectors are, in my opinion, underutilized. Take some time to learn more about them.

For further information about CSS Selectors, pattern matching, and Inheritance, see Adrian Senior's article (www.dwmagic/go/18) and the W3C recommendation for CSS2 on selectors (www.dwmagic/go/19).

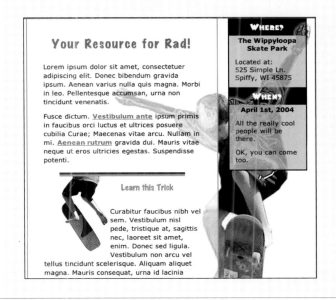

You may have noticed that the body element on the page has an `id` class declared. It says: `<body id="trickpage">`. Here's how it works:

1 Insert the **04–Here CSS** snippet into your page, save it, and view the selectors.

The first selector begins with `body#trickpage div#nav ul li,` and selects any `li` element that is a descendant of an `ul` element that is a descendant of a `<div>` element with an id attribute that equals `nav` that is a descendant of a body element with an id attribute that equals trickpage. Sound confusing? Here's what's happening in plain English. I placed an `id` trickpage on the `<body>` tag of my page about Trick Tips (each page is given a specific `id` on the `<body>` tag that is unique; the selectors for all of them are in the **04–Here CSS** snippet). Then, through the selector, I instructed the page that if there is an `id` of trickpage on the `body` selector, apply this style to the `li` in the `ul` in the nav `<div>`. That style appears the same as the regular `div#nav li` selector for the button.

The second selector begins with `body#trickpage div#nav ul li.tricks a,` and goes one step further. It selects any `a` element that is a descendant of an `li` element with a class attribute named "tricks" that is a descendant of an `ul` element that is a descendant of a `<div>` element with an id attribute that equals `nav` that is a descendant of a body element with an id attribute that equals trickpage. What that one means in plain English is that if there is an `a` element with the `id` tricks, on a page where the `<body>` tag has the `id` of trickpage (of course in the nav `<div>` and in a unnumbered list), it should be rendered as it is defined in that selector. That style is exactly like the hover/focus style from the `div#nav li a` selector.

Tip: There's a great resource that helps you decipher complex selectors. Use it often, and you'll soon understand these selectors at a glance. It's called the SelectOracle (www.dwmagic.com/go/20). You input complicated selectors into the form, click "Explain This," and it will give you their meaning. It's an invaluable tool for learning.

2 Now you can experiment with this technique. Do a "Save As" on your index page, create a couple new pages, and give them different names. Go into each page and give the body `id` one of the `ids` I've created in the **04–Here CSS** snippet (linkspage, tourpage, gallerypage). Now preview them in a browser and notice how the active (black background) button changes from page to page dependant on the body ID given.

3 Validate your pages. Get in the habit of validating both your HTML (XHTML) and CSS. This will save you time and headache because you will have fewer problems if you are coding to standards. Yep, there will probably always be the occasional CSS hack you'll have to use when a browser just can't get it right, but you'll be way ahead of the game. Use Dreamweaver's built-in validation (File > Check Page > Validate Markup) or the W3C site. (Validate your CSS at `www.dwmagic.com/go/22` and validate your HTML and XHTML at `www.dwmagic.com/go/23`.)

Note: I haven't discussed support for Netscape 4 type browsers in this project. If you need to support Netscape 4, there's a simple hack to hide styles from it. For me, it's much easier to keep all my styles in one linked CSS document and hide the things that give Netscape 4 trouble. John Gallant and Holly Bergevin wrote an excellent article on the Caio Hack (www.dwmagic.com/go/21).

For tips on debugging your CSS layouts, read Holly Bergevin's "Debugging CSS the Easy Way" article at www.dwmagic.com/go/24.

Now Try This

By now you've learned how to use a method of *Tromp l'oeil* that makes the viewer believe they are seeing through certain elements on your page, how to use the CSS to really take control of your page, and how to show a different button style to indicate which page the user is on without any server-side code or JavaScript—only CSS.

Here are some ideas on how to apply the skills you've learned or use the project you've completed in other ways:

• It's sometimes preferable to control the line length of your content area. If you don't want to have a fluid content section, you can define the width of the content `<div>` and give it percentage-based left and right margins to keep it in the middle of the page.

• Experiment with different button end caps and images for `<div>` corners, from simple funky shapes to gradients. There's no limit to what you can do. Don't be satisfied with square, mundane styling. Jazz it up!

Creating Toggle-O-Matic Menus

Angela C. Buraglia

Angela C. Buraglia is perhaps best known as the founder of DreamweaverFAQ.com, a site dedicated to serving the Dreamweaver community which she continues to run today with Daniel Short. She is also the co-author of *Dreamweaver MX 2004 Killer Tips* and *Dreamweaver MX Killer Tips* with Joseph Lowery.

Dan Short and I were faced with redesigning DWfaq.com, and neither of us were happy with our navigational system because it wasn't very user friendly and had some design flaws. When Dreamweaver MX came out, we took one look and realized that the Panel groups would make a nice little menu system, one that any Dreamweaver user could relate to and navigate easily. I liked the menus so much that I started using them on DWmommy.com almost immediately.

When I saw Dreamweaver MX 2004, I thought about changing the menus to look like its Panel groups instead, but the Dreamweaver MX style had grown on me already. Anyway, the look of Toggle-O-Matic menus is entirely configurable with CSS, which is one reason why I really love these menus. So if your heart desires, you can style your Toggle-O-Matic menus to look like the Panel groups in Dreamweaver MX 2004, or you can find a style of your very own.

It Works Like This

Toggle-O-Matic menus are so simple, fast, and chic that you'll find yourself toggling submenus over and over again just for fun. How the menus look is entirely up to you; they're all CSS-driven. Simply put, the CSS display property is set to `none` and switched to `block` by way of some crafty little JavaScript. The purpose of this project is to familiarize you with the possibilities. I won't be getting into CSS specifics other than what you need to know to create the toggle effect. After all, how you style your buttons is up to you. You can make the menu buttons and submenus any color, size, font, and so on that suits your needs. Here are the basic steps of the project:

1   Style menu buttons and submenus with CSS and then toggle the submenu's display property with the Toggle Menu extension.

2   Swap classes with the Toggle Class extension to set a menu button to a down state. Not to worry—all JavaScript is added painlessly via the Toggle Menus and Toggle Class extensions.

3   Set a specific submenu to open automatically when the page has loaded using the Toggle Menus extension.

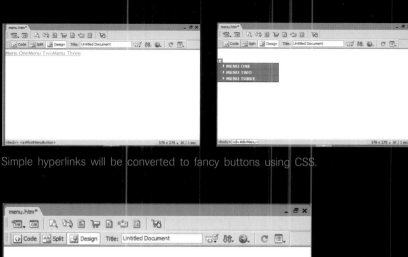

Simple hyperlinks will be converted to fancy buttons using CSS.

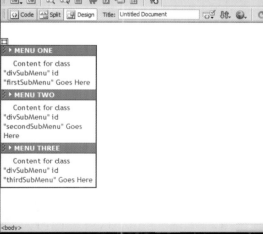

Using design-time CSS you'll be able to modify the content of your submenus visually in Design view.

Preparing to Work

To prepare for this project, you will need to do the following:

1   Install both the **Toggle Menu.mxp** and **Toggle Link Class.mxp** extensions (both are behaviors). See Appendix A, "Installing Extensions," for more information.

2   Copy the **Projects/02** folder from the CD to your hard drive. Define a new site using the Projects/02 copy as your site root.

3   Take a look at **finished.htm** (in the **finished** folder of the project) in every browser that you have. Depending on which browsers you used, you may have noticed that the menus look just a little bit different. You've done something that nobody else—other than perhaps your client—will do.

    To help you follow along, I'll be using some very consistent naming conventions. When I say *menu button*, I mean that which you click on that will expose the submenu. It needn't be button-shaped just because of its name. In code, *MenuButton* and *SubMenu* will be used as suffixes so that you can easily see the relationships between the elements. Don't worry, it will make sense once you get into the project.

4   Create a new HTML page.

5   In the Basic Page category, select HTML. I prefer to always make my new documents XHTML Compliant. So if you're a stickler like me, check the XHTML box in the lower-right corner.

6   Save the file as menu.htm.

Browser Compatibility

Toggle-O-Matic Menus has been tested for functionality in the following browsers:

- Microsoft Internet Explorer 5.0 (Windows and Macintosh)
- Microsoft Internet Explorer 5.5 (Windows)
- Microsoft Internet Explorer 6 (Windows)
- Netscape 6 and 7 (Windows and Macintosh)

Forging Friendly Hyperlinks to Submenus

There's nothing fancy about making these menu buttons. Sure they look fancy, but the code is just a simple link. You might be thinking that a simple hyperlink will load a page in the browser when all you really want to do is expand the submenu. As long as JavaScript is enabled, the hyperlink will not be followed; the user will not leave the current page while he toggles submenus with the menu buttons. The Toggle Menu extension takes care of preventing your menu button hyperlinks from loading (if JavaScript is indeed enabled). Right now I want you to know that by providing a real hyperlink, as opposed to a null hyperlink such as javascript:; or #, it provides several benefits:

- If JavaScript happens to be turned off, the hyperlink you use could take the user to another page where the submenu is visible so that the user can navigate the site as intended.

- Search engines can follow real hyperlinks, but hyperlinks in behavior actions are not followed. Search engines can't follow a null hyperlink.

- When users place their pointers over the hyperlink, they'll see an actual file path in their browser's status bar. Some people are suspicious of clicking a hyperlink if they can't see where you'll be taking them (as in the case of a null hyperlink).

With those benefits in mind, it's time to get started:

1   Select the Hyperlink object found in the Common category of the Insert bar, or choose Insert > Hyperlink.

Tip: Set up a keyboard shortcut (Edit > Keyboard Shortcuts) for Insert > Hyperlink to get to the Hyperlink dialog even quicker. There's a Help button at the bottom of the Keyboard Shortcuts dialog if you get stuck.

---

2   Complete the Hyperlink dialog. For this project, Text and Link are the only two fields you need to complete, but if you'd like to do the rest, you're welcome. Give the menu button whatever text you like. In the demo, I used Menu One.

3   Repeat steps 1 and 2 for as many menu buttons as you intend to have.

I added two more menus: Menu Two and Menu Three. Right now, you should have one hyperlink directly after the next in Design or Code view. They look like plain, boring blue underlined hyperlinks, but they won't for much longer.

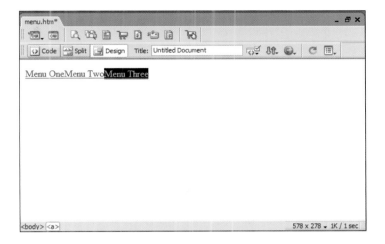

4   Click the Attach Style Sheets icon in the lower-right corner of the CSS Styles panel (Window > CSS Styles).

5   Click the Browse button in the Link External Stylesheet dialog, then locate and select **menus.css** in the root of your project folder.

6   Set Add As to Link, and click OK. Alright, so that isn't much of an improvement. You'll get there soon. I promise.

7   Save your work.

Time to Identify: *ID* Attributes for Menu Buttons

Each menu button requires a unique id attribute that will be used in the JavaScript that toggles the submenus. This is the easiest way to add an id to the hyperlinks you've already created:

1   If the Tag inspector isn't visible, choose Window > Tag Inspector or press the F9 keyboard shortcut.

2   If it is not already visible, select the Attributes tab of the Tag inspector.

> **Note:** The Tag inspector's panel group name includes the tag you've selected, in this case <a>. I find this helpful because it lets me know that I have the right HTML element selected.

3   Click on the first Menu Button hyperlink in Design view.

4   If it isn't already shown, change the Tag inspector to the Show List view by clicking the Show List View icon.

> **Note:** If you prefer the Show Category view, you'll find id listed there too, under the CSS/Accessibility section. I find the Show List view quick and easy, because I can see all attributes at a glance, sorted alphabetically.

5   In the right column, across from the id attribute, type in a unique id for the selected hyperlink. Call the first one firstMenuButton.

Remember, I told you near the beginning of the chapter that you'll be using MenuButton as a suffix for all references to menu buttons? Next, you'll need to add the id attribute to the remaining two menu button hyperlinks.

6   Click on the next menu button hyperlink in Design view.

7   Assign the hyperlink a unique id as you did in step 5. Use an id of secondMenuButton. Click on the third menu button hyperlink and assign an id of thirdMenuButton.

8   Save your document.

Getting Classified

It's about time to start making these buttons look pretty. You just need to apply a custom class from the provided style sheet to each of the menu buttons. The custom class is called aMenuButton. The a is for anchor or <a>, which is the type of tag that you're going to apply this custom class to. I like to give custom classes names like that to help me remember their purpose if they're used for no other element. For each menu button you perform the following steps:

1   Click on the first Menu Button in Design view.

2   Right-click/Ctrl-click the <a> tag in the tag selector.

3   Select Set Class > aMenuButton. Do the same for the second and third menu buttons.

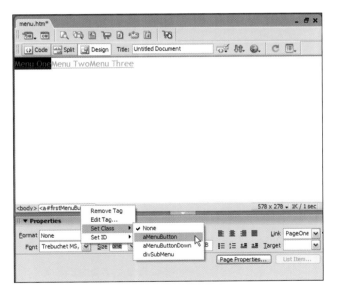

4   Save your work.

Note: It is very important that the aMenuButton class is applied to the <a> tags. Even though you don't have any other tags in the document <body> yet, it is possible that Dreamweaver will wrap the tags with a <span> or <p> tag if you apply the CSS by other methods than described in the steps.

Containing the Menu with *<div>* Tags

Things still aren't looking pretty yet. That's because the navigation hyperlinks are defined to use the descendant selector #divMenu a.menuButton. This means that only anchors with a class of aMenuButton within an element identified as divMenu will be styled the way you've defined. Using a descendant selector allows you to give only the buttons inside your navigation layer the fancy styling you're after. You already have all the anchors using the aMenuButton class; now put them inside a <div>. First you'll add tags to contain the entire Toggle-O-Matic menu system. In the next section, you'll add the <div> tags for the submenus.

1   In Design view, select all three menu button hyperlinks.

2   In the Layout category of the Insert bar, click the Insert Div Tag icon.

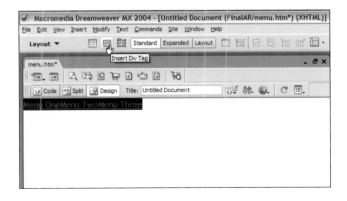

3   Leave the Class field blank. In the ID drop-down, select `divMenu`, which is the only available `id` defined in the CSS file.

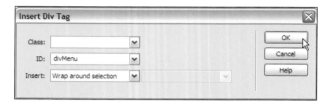

Tip: Only unused `id`s are made available in the ID drop-down list. If you've used that `id` on the page once before, it will be removed from the list to help ensure that your `id`s are unique to the page.

4   Make sure Insert is set to Wrap Around Selection, and click OK. Choosing Wrap Around Selection will ensure that all of your hyperlinks are placed inside the newly inserted `<div>`.

5   Save your work.

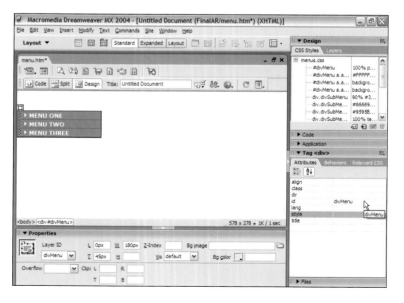

Inserting Submenu *<div>* Tags

You now have beautifully styled menu buttons. Don't get caught up on what the CSS means or does yet. I'll explain all that in a section near the end of the project. The important thing to note is things are taking shape now, and you're more than halfway done. Now, add the three submenus using the following steps for each:

1   Click the Insert Div Tag icon (it doesn't matter where your cursor is).

2   Choose divSubMenu from the Class drop-down list because this time you're adding a submenu.

Tip: If you don't already have `id`s defined for every element you want to use, you can add them anyway through the Insert DIV Tag dialog. Don't see an `id` you want? Simply type it into the dialog anyway.

3   Give the first submenu an `id` of firstSubMenu. Because this `id` isn't specified in your stylesheet, just type it in.

4   In the Insert drop-down, choose After Tag and select `<a id="firstMenuButton">` from the List menu. This inserts each submenu after its respective menu button.

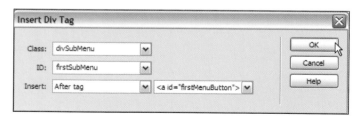

5   Click OK.

Note: Don't be alarmed because you don't see any submenus in Design view. You'll be able to edit your submenus after you've completed the next section.

6   Do the same for the second and third menus, using <u>secondSubMenu</u> and <u>thirdSubMenu</u> as the value in the ID field. Be sure to insert them after their respective menu buttons.

7   Save your work.

Design Time CSS to the Rescue

With `div.divSubMenu` in menus.css set to `display:none;`, you won't be able to see the submenus in Design view. If you're inclined to do so, you're more than welcome to edit the submenus in Code view, but it will be easier in Design view. You could modify menus.css while you're working every time you need to see submenus, but that would be a hassle. Instead you can take advantage of Dreamweaver's Design Time Style Sheets feature.

Design Time Style Sheets are invisibly attached to a document via a Design Note. Have you ever wondered what those _notes folders with .mno files are doing in your site? Well, Design Time Style Sheet info is but one of their purposes. In dtMenus.css you'll find `div.divSubMenu` set to `display: block !important;`. The `!important` property makes the Design Time Style Sheet take priority over the regularly linked style sheet, making the sub-menus visible for editing.

1   Choose Window > CSS Styles or Shift+F11.

2   Choose Options > Design-time. The icon in the right corner of the expanded panel with the three little lines and a down arrow is called the Options menu.

3   When the Design Time Style Sheets dialog appears, click the (+) button above Show Only at Design Time.

4   Browse to **dtMenus.css**.

5   Click OK.

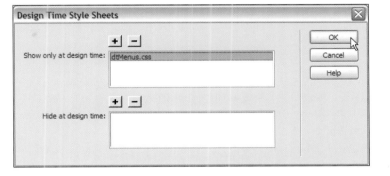

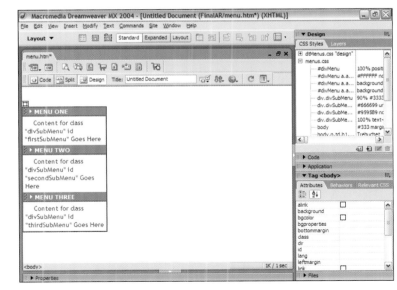

CSS Requirements

I've made it real easy for you by providing the working CSS files. If you want to create your own menu button and submenu styles, there are only a few things you need to know that are required for the Toggle-O-Matic menu system to work.

Menu Buttons

In this project, the custom class for menu buttons is called a.aMenuButton. For the hyperlinks to stack upon each other vertically, you need to have `display: block;` in the menu button's class declaration. This tells the browser to display the hyperlink as a block-level element instead of its default, which is inline.

If you'd like to have another style for menu buttons when their submenu is exposed, you'll need to have a separate custom class. You'll find a.aMenuButtonDown defined in menus.css for that purpose. Typically, all you'd change here are any colors and the background image.

Listing 2.1

```
/* Menu Button Styles */
#divMenu a.aMenuButton, #divMenu a.aMenuButtonDown {
    background-color: #7B83B5;
    border: 1px solid #5B667B;
    border-top: none;
    padding: 2px 0px 2px 25px;
    font: bold small-caps 80% Verdana, Arial, Helvetica,
    sans-serif;
    color: #FFFFFF;
    text-decoration: none;
    background-repeat: no-repeat;
    background-position: 3px 50%;
    display: block;
}
/* Set menu button's image */
#divMenu a.aMenuButton {
    background-image: url(assets/images/inactive.gif);
}
/* Change menu button's image on hover and when down */
```

```
#divMenu a.aMenuButton:hover, #divMenu a.aMenuButtonDown {
    background-image: url(assets/images/expand.gif);
}

/* Submenu Styles */
div.divSubMenu {
    background:#FFFFFF;
    color:#333333;
    text-indent: 18px;
    padding: 5px;
    border: 1px solid #5B667B;
    font-size:90%;
    display: none;
}
```

Submenus

The custom class for the submenus, div.divSubMenu, needs to have `display: none;` in its style declaration. By setting the display property to none, you will be hiding the submenus both in Design view and the browser. Because you can't see the submenus while you work in Dreamweaver's Design view, you have a Design Time Style Sheet (dtMenus.css) that contains div.divSubMenu set to `display:block!important;`.

Note: Keep in mind that none of these custom classes should have any positioning properties. The elements need to be relative to each other so that the elements below the submenus are moved as the menus are toggled and not covered up.

Toggling with Extensions

This part is going to be very easy. In this section you'll apply two extensions to each of the menu button hyperlinks. The first one, Toggle Menu, uses JavaScript to check the display property of the specified submenu. If it is set to none, then it switches it to block and vice versa. The second behavior you'll apply is Toggle Link Class, which switches the style of the menu button (`a.aMenuButton`) to its down state (`a.aMenuButtonDown`).

Tip: It is a good idea to work in Code and Design view at the same time so that you can make selections in Design view while having the code in Code view while you use the extensions. You'll need to know the selected menu button's `id` for this part, and you'll have to cancel out of the dialog to find it if you can't remember and you don't have it in front of you.

---

1   While selecting the menu button hyperlink in Design view, click the (+) Add Behavior button in the Behaviors panel (Window > Behaviors or Shift+F3) and select DWfaq > Toggle Menu to bring up the Toggle Menu dialog.

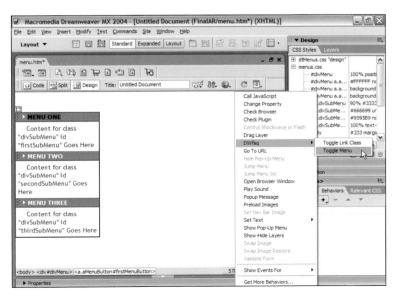

2   Click the listed submenu `id` that corresponds to the menu button you've selected. Click the Select button. You should see (`Selected`) appear beside the submenu's name. Click OK.

3   Verify that the event has been set to onClick in the Behaviors panel. If the behaviors have not been set to onClick, be sure to change them by choosing onClick from the list menu in the Behaviors panel.

Tip: You can apply the same Toggle Menu and Toggle Link Class behaviors to the `<body>` tag onLoad to display a submenu when the page loads. For extra fun, create a Toggle All hyperlink and select every layer in the Toggle Class extension. It's possible to choose more than one `<div>` at a time in the extension.

Note: If onClick is not listed as an option, click the (+) Add Behavior button in the Behaviors panel and select Show Events For > 4.0 and Later Browsers.

---

4   While selecting the menu button hyperlink in Design view, click the (+) Add Behavior button in the Behaviors panel (Window > Behaviors) and select DWfaq > Toggle Link Class. In the Toggle Menu dialog that appears, you'll see a list of Elements that have `id` attributes defined.

5   Click the menu button's id in the list and select the class for the menu button's down state, aMenuButtonDown, and click OK.

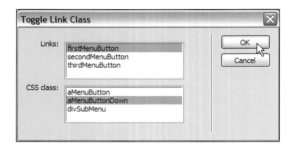

6   Be sure that the event listed for Toggle Link Class is set to onClick.

7   Repeat steps 1 through 5 for each menu button.

8   Save your work.

Tip: You may consider using a Dreamweaver Library Item to contain the Toggle-O-Matic menu system so that when you need to do updates, you just modify one file and Dreamweaver will update all files that use the Library Item for you.

If you have access to a server that can process Server Side Includes, I would advise using SSIs so that you can upload just the menu file, rather than all files that use the menu when you do updates. For information on how to use SSI, see Daniel Short's tutorial at www.dwmagic.com/go/12.

Now Try This

By now you've learned how to style menu buttons and submenus with CSS. You've also learned how to toggle the submenu's display property with the Toggle Menu extension, swap classes with the Toggle Class extension to set a menu button to a down state, and last, how to set a submenu to open automatically when the page has loaded.

Here are some ideas on how to apply the skills you've learned or use the project you've completed in other ways:

- In all actuality, you're not limited to creating menus with the techniques you've learned in this project. For example, you could create an FAQ (Frequently Asked Questions) list that displays only the questions as links, and then the answers could be toggled beneath them. Take a look at **faq.htm** in the **NowTryThis** folder for an example. You'll notice that only the Toggle Menu's extension was used for this example. You could take it further by using the Toggle Link Class extension, as well.

- If it's another menu system you're after, try creating a tree/file menu system. This look can be achieved using styled bulleted lists instead of <div> tags. Take a few minutes to examine the code in **treemenu.htm** inside the **NowTryThis** folder to see one way this type of menu can be achieved.

PROJECT 3

Managing Navigation Button States in Template-Controlled Sites

Murray R. Summers

Murray R. Summers is a Macromedia Certified Web Site Developer and Dreamweaver Developer, and has authored several books, including the premier treatment of advanced Template properties, *Dreamweaver MX Templates*, with Brad Halstead.

Ever since co-authoring a book about Templates in Dreamweaver MX with Brad Halstead (and having a great time doing it!), the use of templates in site development has become my passion. Yet I sense that there are many users of Dreamweaver MX who have not made these discoveries about "advanced templating," and so I want to try to introduce them to these concepts without burying them in the details.

One of the most fascinating things about Dreamweaver (to me, at least) is the surprise-filled nooks and crannies one can find in it. Having found these, used them, and discovered the new capabilities or power they convey in your site development makes it hard not to "gush" about them. One of these remarkably robust discoveries for me was the new template capabilities introduced in Dreamweaver MX. So, I picked a topic for this chapter that has—what seems to me—universal appeal (the notion of setting a navigation button's down state to indicate page location), and that allows a very simple introduction of this advanced template capability. It is my hope that this tiny peek at template optional regions (and the underlying widgets that make them work) will stimulate your curiosity to explore further.

It Works Like This

The goal for this chapter is to produce Template child pages on which you can easily control the button showing the down state. On the way, you also will learn how to remove the rollover and the hyperlink from the button on each child page. Here are the basic steps of the project:

1   Initialize the page by placing up state button images into Editable Regions of the Template.

2   Use JavaScript code to dynamically set the button's image source. It will do this based on variables whose values are exposed in Editable Regions and can be set on the Template's child pages.

3   Use Template Optional Regions to determine which button state to show.

These images show how to initialize the page and use JavaScript to dynamically set the button's image source.

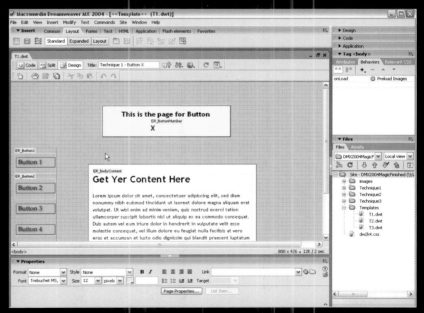

Here you're using Template Optional Regions to determine which button state to show.

Preparing to Work

To prepare for this project, you will need to do the following:

1   Look on the accompanying CD-ROM in the **Projects\03** folder to see the project file structure.

2   Install the extension **Project 03 Snippets.mxp.** See Appendix A, "Installing Extensions," for details.

3   Copy the contents of the accompanying CD-ROM folder **Projects\03\Working_Files** to a new folder named **Project_03** on your local hard drive.

4   Start Dreamweaver and create a site definition pointing to the **Project_03** folder that you created in step 3. Name the site Project 03.

Note: Each technique is unique yet able to be applied to any design you may create that employs Dreamweaver MX 2004 Templates. Each of these techniques will be discussed individually. If one method really floats your boat, please jump to that section and perform its steps. There is no requirement to do these techniques in any order, although I have taught from easiest to most complex. Now have at it!

Using Editable Regions

Note: This technique is completely compatible with Macromedia Contribute.

The very simplest way to make specific menu buttons stay down on child pages is to make each button into a Template Editable Region. This enables you to adjust the source file and link information for each button on its associated child page.

1   Open the file **Templates\T1.dwt** by double-clicking it in the Files panel and select Split view (View > Code and Design).

2   Select Button 1 in the navigation menu on the left, and then click on the <a> tag in the Tag selector (to make sure your next step wraps the <a> tag). Finally, right-click/Ctrl-click on the selected area in Design view and choose Templates > New Editable Region from the Context menu.

3   Name the new Editable Region ER_Button1, and click OK. Notice that the Editable Region automatically wraps the anchor tag that is already assigned to the image. This will work to your advantage as you'll see in step 9.

4   Repeat steps 2 and 3 for Button 2, using the name <u>ER_Button2</u>.

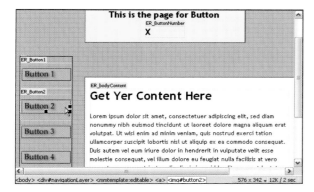

5   Save the template.

6   In the Update Template Files dialog that appears (showing the already created instance or child pages), click Update. The Update Pages dialog opens and performs the update to the child pages of this template.

7   When the update is completed and you've verified in the report that all files have been updated, click Close to close the Update Pages dialog.

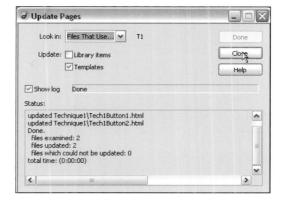

8   Close the template and open the file named **Technique1\ Tech1Button1.html**.

9   Select Button 1 and use the Property inspector's Browse icon for the Src field to select **button1_d.jpg** as the source file for the button's down state. Clear the Link field to remove the behaviors and link associated with the button. Click the cautionary message OK button to acknowledge the removal of the behaviors.

10   Save the file and preview it.

11   Repeat steps 8 through 10 for the file **Technique1\
Tech1Button2.html**, selecting Button 2 and using **button2_d.jpg**
for the down state's source image. (Don't forget to clear the link field
for this button, too!)

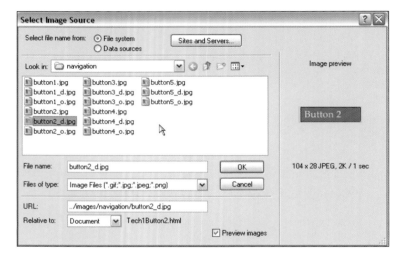

12   Using the Files panel, select **Technique1\Tech1Button1.html** and
press F12 to preview it in your default browser. Press Buttons 1, then
2, then 1 and make sure that the button states change with the page
change. You should see the appropriate down-state buttons on the
pages. If there are any open files, close them.

Note: Perhaps the largest disadvantage of this method is that none of
your image source attributes are contained within non-editable parts of
the Template code. This means that the possibility exists to inadvertently
use the Button 6 down image for the Button 2 source or that the
dimensions of this image could be inadvertently changed, with attendant
undesirable layout consequences. Another disadvantage is that there
is no way to control or propagate the link for the buttons. As you
progress through this project, you'll take care of all these problems.

Using JavaScript and Editable Regions

Note: This technique is not suitable for use in Macromedia Contribute
because it relies on your ability to access JavaScript code in the child
pages' Editable Region, and Contribute cannot easily edit at the code
level.

Next in the order of complexity is a way to use a tiny bit of JavaScript to
dynamically write the source attribute for a given button to the down state.
This technique solves one of the disadvantages mentioned in the previous
section. Here, the image source statements are all contained in non-
editable parts of the Template page. This method introduces a drawback
though: the inability to remove the hyperlink for the down state button.

1   Using the Files panel, open the file **Templates\T2.dwt** and select
Split view (View > Code and Design).

2   In Code view, click to position your cursor immediately before the
closing </body> tag. Now, return focus to Design view by clicking on
the scroll bar. Confirm that your insertion point is now active within
Design view (it is flashing), and then press the Return/Enter key three
times to insert three paragraphs.

This moves the cursor below the content area so that you can see what you're doing. Your code should look like this:

Listing 3.1

```
<!-- TemplateEndEditable --></div>
<p> </p>
<p> </p>
<p> </p>
</body>
</html>
```

3   With your cursor positioned in the last paragraph, right-click/ Ctrl-click and select Templates > New Editable Region from the context menu. Name this Editable Region ER_javascriptVariables, and click OK.

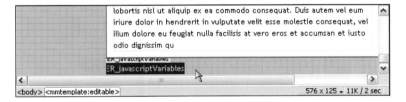

You are going to create variables to be used by a tiny snippet of JavaScript in the head of the Template and child documents. This JavaScript will dynamically write the down state of the button after the page loads. To enable you to change those variables on each child page, you will put the variable declarations in the Editable Region that you just created.

4   Locate the ER_javascriptVariables Editable Region you just created in Code view. Select the placeholder text for that region and replace it with the code indicated here (or use the snippet **MX Magic 2004 > Project 03 > 02–Body_Javascript**).

Listing 3.2

```
<script type="text/JavaScript">
<!--
  var msobj="";
  var msurl="";
//-->
</script>
```

5   While still in Code view, locate the start of the first JavaScript function declaration in the <head> block and place your cursor just after this code snippet:

Listing 3.3

```
<script language="JavaScript" type="text/JavaScript">
<!--
```

6   Insert the function declaration shown here (or use the snippet **MX Magic 2004 > Project 03 > 01–Head_Javascript**):

Listing 3.4

```
function MS_downImage() {
var ms1;
if ((ms1=MM_findObj(msobj))!=null) {ms1.src=msurl;}
}
```

7   In the Template page, add an onLoad event handler to the <body> tag by locating the <body> tag (approximately line 44) and changing the tag to the code shown here (or use the snippet **MX Magic 2004 > Project 03 > 03–Body_onload_call**):

Listing 3.5

```
<body onLoad="MS_downImage()">
```

This onLoad event handler calls MS_downImage(), the JavaScript function you added in step 6.

8   Save the Template, update the child pages when prompted, and close them using Ctrl+W/Cmd+W.

Normally at this point you would create two new pages, modify the title of each, and save each to the appropriate folder. Because this is rather redundant, you'll skip that part and head right into updating the already generated files.

Note: The JavaScript block in the ER_javascriptVariables Editable Region of the template made it on to the child pages. This is because you added the new Editable Region, inserted the code, saved the template, and then updated the pages. Normally, Editable Region content does not propagate to child pages once the Editable Region exists on the child page.

---

9   Open **Technique2\Tech2Button1.html** using the Files panel. In Code view, scroll to about line 70 and change the var statements for msobj and msurl as shown here before saving:

Listing 3.6

```
var msobj="button1";
var msurl="../images/navigation/button1_d.jpg";
```

This tells the page's JavaScript function to find the button named (with the id) button1 and set its src attribute to the down state image button1_d.jpg.

10   Repeat step 9 for the second child page (**Technique2\ Tech2Button2.html**), using button2 and ../images/navigation/ button2_d.jpg, respectively, in the variable declarations.

11   Save and close all open files, updating if prompted, and preview the file named **Technique2\Tech2Button1.html**.

Note: You have now seen two ways to control button states in Template pages. The technique described in this section has the advantage that the button's source attribute is now located in the Template's Non-Editable Region. Template-level changes to navigation file locations or file/pathnames that you specified in the ER_javascriptVariables Editable Region will *not* propagate to all child pages. You still have a rollover on the down-state image, however, and a redundant link. The third technique manages both of these problems.

Using Optional Regions

It's time to take a small step into the world of Dreamweaver's advanced Template features. In this technique, *both* the up and the down state buttons will exist on the template. You will make each of these buttons into Template Optional Regions, which allow independent control of their display on child pages. By doing this, you can eliminate both the rollover and the links on the buttons.

1   Using the Files panel, open the file **Templates\T3.dwt**.

2 Using Design view, select the Line Break shield beside Button 1 and press the left arrow on the keyboard. This will move your cursor to the left of the line break (
 tag) and position it to receive the image for the button's down state without it being in the anchor (<a> tag) for the existing Button 1.

Note: If you don't see the Line Break shield, edit your Preferences (Ctrl+U/Cmd+U), choose the Invisible Elements Category, check Line Breaks, and then click OK in the Preferences dialog. Also, choose View > Visual Aids > Invisible Elements and make sure there is a check beside it. If not, then select it and the check will appear. You should now have no problems viewing the Line Break shield.

3 Select Insert > Image. Browse to and select the down state image for Button 1 (**button1_d.jpg**).

You will now have both buttons in that part of the menu: the up and down button for Button 1.

4 Select the down image for Button 1, and name it <u>button1d</u> using the Property inspector's name field (it's not labeled), tabbing out of the field to set the value. Right-click/Ctrl-click on the button1d image to open the context menu, and select Templates > New Optional Region.

An Optional Region is used around this image to control its inclusion in the child page. This, in turn, is controlled by a template parameter that is automatically inserted when an Optional Region is added to the page.

5 In the New Optional Region dialog, choose the Basic tab and enter OR_Button1Down in the Name field. Clear the Show by Default check box, and click OK to close the dialog.

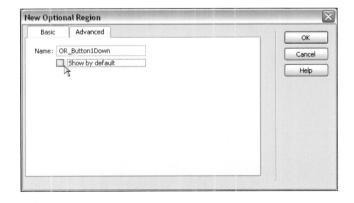

You have just created a Template Parameter (OR_Button1Down), an Optional Region that is controlled by the value given to the Template Parameter, and set a default of false for that parameter. This means that if you spawn a child page from this Template file, that downstate image will *not* be shown. In fact, the code for it is not even written into the child page.

6   Select the image named button1, choose Insert > Template Objects > Optional Region. Choose the Advanced tab, click on the Enter Expression radio button, and enter !OR_Button1Down in the text area. Click OK. Save the Template page and update the child pages when prompted.

The Template Expression you just entered, !OR_Button1Down, tests the value of the parameter OR_Button1Down. If the value is false in the child page, then that child page will contain the code for the up state of Button 1. If the value is true in the child page, then the child page will contain the code for the down state of Button 1.

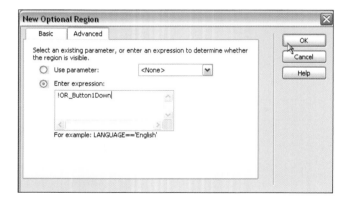

7   Repeat steps 2 through 6 for Button 2. Use OR_Button2Down for the Optional Region name assigned to Button 2 and !OR_Button2Down for the Expression's value assigned to Button 2's Optional Region. Save the template, update pages if prompted, and close the template.

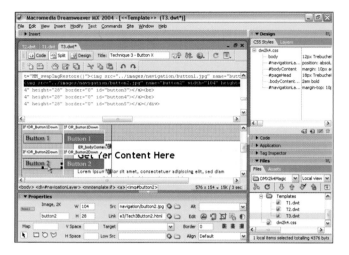

8   Open **Technique3\Button1.html** and select Modify > Template Properties. Select the OR_Button1Down parameter in the text area, and check the check box for Show OR_Button1Down. Click the OK button to close the Template Properties dialog and see the changes you made in Design and Code views. Save the page. When you preview the page, you should see the down state for Button 1.

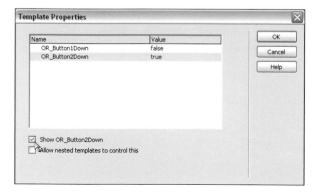

9   Repeat step 8 for **Technique3\Tech3Button2.html**, this time setting the OR_Button2Down parameter to true by selecting the check box for Show OR_Button2Down.

10 Save the page, and preview it.

An Explanation of the Elements

Note: This technique is completely compatible with Macromedia Contribute because all template parameters in all child pages are exposed through Contribute's user interface.

How does this magic work? It relies on two of Dreamweaver MX 2004's advanced Template features: Template Parameters and Template Expressions.

1   In Code view for **Templates\T3.dwt**, find this code at roughly line 36:

Listing 3.7

```
<!-- TemplateBeginEditable name="head" -->
➡<!-- TemplateEndEditable -->
➡<!--TemplateParam name="OR_Button1Down"
➡type="boolean" value="false" -->
➡<!--TemplateParam name="OR_Button2Down"
➡type="boolean" value="false" -->
```

This code shows two Template parameter definitions (OR_Button1Down and OR_Button2Down). These parameters are used to control the presence/absence of the two corresponding Optional Regions (with the same names as these parameters), based on the expressions you entered during the Optional Region creation in step 6. Your assigned default values for these parameters are used in each child page until you change them. Because these lines are in a non-editable part of the Template page, they will be propagated to all derived child pages.

When you spawn a child page and then use Modify > Template Properties (Format > Template Properties in Contribute), you are changing these values as written to the page, and as used by Dreamweaver in determining which Optional Region to display.

2   Consider the resulting code in the **Technique3\Tech3Button1.html** child page shown here:

Listing 3.8

```
<!-- InstanceBeginEditable name="head" -->
➡<!-- InstanceEndEditable -->
➡<!--InstanceParam name="OR_Button1Down"
➡type="boolean" value="true" -->
➡<!--InstanceParam name="OR_Button2Down"
➡type="boolean" value="false" -->
```

Notice that the value of OR_Button1Down has been changed from false to true. This is what you did in the child page, in step 9, by using the Template Properties dialog.

CAUTION

Do not change these values in the child page markup or they will have no effect. The dialog referenced (Modify > Template Properties) must always be used to change the template parameters in a child page.

---

3   Look at the page code of **Templates\T3.dwt** for the button1 and button1d images (approximately line number 41) to find the two code phrases shown here:

Listing 3.9

```
<!-- TemplateBeginIf cond="!OR_Button1Down" -->
<!-- TemplateBeginIf cond="_document['OR_Button1Down']" -->
```

In the first line, if the condition is true (`OR_Button1Down` is equal to false), then the code for the button's up state is written to the child page (`<img src="../images/navigation/button1.jpg">`). The second line tests for the down state of the button. If the Template parameter (`OR_Button1Down`) is true, then the code for the down button is written to the child page (`<img src="../images/navigation/button1_d.jpg">`).

Note: If you carefully examine the child pages of the Templates used in this section, you will notice that code contained in a failed conditional test is not echoed into the child pages, and the Template-specific markup that defines these tests is also not echoed to the child pages.

The result of this is not only "bloat" control on the child pages, but also a barrier to reverse-engineering the parent Template page from a child page.

Note: In the downstate button page, that button's image is not wrapped with the anchor tag, and therefore is not a redundant hyperlink.

Now Try This

By now you've learned how to place button images into Editable Regions of the Template, use JavaScript code to dynamically set the button's image source, and use Template Optional Regions to determine which button state to show.

Here are some ideas on how to apply the skills you've learned or use the project you've completed in other ways:

- The obvious modification to the last method (using Optional Regions) is to extend it to cover text-based navigation. And in fact, that is relatively easy.

- Instead of using Optional Regions to write image rollovers and hyperlinks, you can use them to write changing class names on navigation text. In other words, you could have a test that writes a span tag with one class for the down state and a different class for the linked up state of the text "buttons."

- Use a template Repeat Region and its variables, and complex expressions (Conditional Operator) to control navigational elements. Consult Project 4, "Controlling Navigation Elements with Templates," for help.

Note: Although the Optional Region markup gives you a glimpse into the kind of power you might discover, these techniques only scratch the surface of the use of Template parameters and Template expressions. If you would like to learn more about how these interesting and powerful tools can change your use of Templates, check out `www.dreamweavermx-templates.com`.

Controlling Navigation Elements with Templates

Brad Halstead

Brad Halstead plays an active roll in the support forums for Dreamweaver, Contribute, and Project Seven. He is HTML 4.01 Certified. Recently, Brad co-authored *Dreamweaver MX Templates* and has been accepted as a Team Macromedia Member for Contribute.

While providing support for Contribute 1.0 and 2.0, I noticed that there was no method of creating accessible links in navigational elements of the page. Because it's important that the navigational elements be accessible, I had to figure out a way of enforcing that—hence this project.

Web site accessibility is one of those Internet buzzwords that isn't. It *is* important (depending on the site) that the page be available to not only fully mobile people but also to people who unfortunately have usability restrictions.

Developing this project has led me down paths that I have infrequently encountered, and has taught me a great deal about web site accessibility. Hopefully you will be able to employ this technique or develop your own for your Contribute users.

It Works Like This

Dreamweaver and Contribute handle some accessibility issues through preferences and dialogs. Others have to be hand-coded in Dreamweaver using Code view or the Tag inspector (Attributes tab). Most of these features cannot be inserted or manipulated using Macromedia Contribute. Here are the basic steps of the project:

1   Insert and modify the specified meta data tags and editors comment to accept data from template parameters.

2   Convert an existing disjointed submenu system that stays compliant with current specs using Dreamweaver templates and template elements (Editable Regions, Repeating Regions, Parameters, and Expressions) so that the aspects of the submenu elements of the design are controlled.

3   Validate the template for Accessibility, XHTML, and CSS by creating an instance (child) page of the template, uploading it to your server, and validating it using the validation engines you desire.

4   Create the site pages with Contribute by using the proper method of creating a new page from the template.

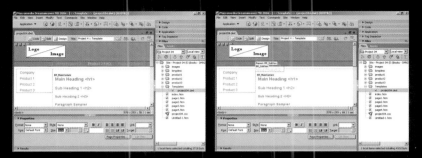

Here you're inserting the specified meta data tags and editors comment to accept data from template parameters.

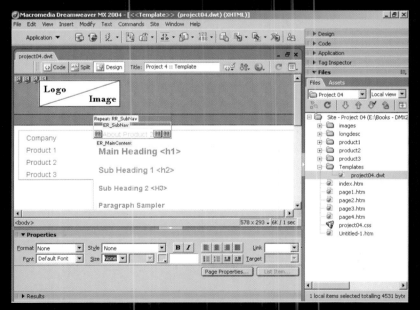

Now two Repeating Region entries are added.

Preparing to Work

To prepare for this project, you will need to do the following:

1 Install the Project 4 snippets extension **Project 04 Snippets.mxp** in the **Projects\04\Extensions** folder. See Appendix A, "Installing Extensions," for instructions.

2 If you're using Dreamweaver MX (6.0 or 6.1), install the Project 4 Strip XML tag extension **StripXMLtag.mxp** in the **Projects\04\Extensions** folder. See Appendix A, "Installing Extensions," for instructions. Please note that you should *not* install this extension if working with Dreamweaver MX 2004!

3 Copy the contents of the accompanying CD-ROM folder **Projects\04\Working_Files** to a new folder named Project_04 on your hard drive.

4 Start Dreamweaver MX 2004 and create a site definition that points to the Project_04 folder; name the site Project 04.

5 Repeat steps 3 and 4 using the CD-ROM folder **Projects\04\ Finished** and the local folder Project_04_F; name the site Project 04 Finished. You can use this as the reference web site for this project.

   The main menu links of the site are root-relative. If you wish to pre-view the site on your local machine, you will need to set up a testing server such as IIS, ColdFusion Server, or Apache and configure your site definition appropriately. Previewing a single page will be fine as long as you don't try to use the main navigational elements. The sub-menu elements work as expected from any previewed page without a testing server.

6 Access the Dreamweaver preferences (Ctrl+U/Cmd+U) and select the Accessibility category. Make sure there is a check in all check boxes. In the Code Rewriting category, make sure there are checks for the top six items and the top radio button is selected. In the Invisible Elements category, ensure there is a check in everything except CSS display:none. In the Validator category, select XHTML 1.0 Strict and uncheck everything else. Leave the Options at their defaults. Click OK to save the changes and close the Preferences dialog.

7 If you have Contribute 1.0 or 2.0 installed, read and follow the instructions found in the file **Projects\04\Extensions\ CT_readme.txt**. Otherwise, skip this step and continue the project as if you were developing for a Contribute user. Be sure to send the **CT_Readme.txt** and **CT_Commands.zip** to your Contribute users or this technique will all be for nothing!

8 Open **ParameterList.pdf**, found in **Projects\04\Extensions**, which contains a breakdown of the finished template's parameters. This document will be useful to you and your clients when you are creating or modifying documents built from the completed template.

Note: Unfortunately, due to a bug in the CSS-P engine, the Template Repeating Region Mini-User Interface (MUI) doesn't function without performing the instructions from step 6.

Browser Compatibility

Employment of this technique is not browser-dependent; however, the design does work well with

- Macromedia Dreamweaver MX (6.1)
- Macromedia Dreamweaver MX 2004 (7.0)
- Macromedia Contribute 1.0
- Macromedia Contribute 2.0
- Internet Explorer 6.0 Service Pack 1 (Windows)
- Mozilla 1.4 (Windows)
- Mozilla Firebird 0.6 (Windows)
- Netscape 6.21, 7.1 (Windows)
- Opera 7.02, 7.11 (Windows)

Controlling Document Meta Data

You will modify the base Dreamweaver template in this section of the project. Before you add display content, you must configure the template's base structure by

- Converting the editor comment to accept a modified date
- Converting the Meta Author tag to be customizable
- Adding editable meta keywords and description tags

You will be performing these conversions and additions by employing template parameters and expressions mostly through the use of the Make Attribute Editable dialog. Follow these steps:

1 Make sure that the Project 04 site is selected, and use the Files panel (F8) to open the template named **project04.dwt** in the **Templates** folder.

2 Select the Split button (Show Code and Design views) so that you can see both the code and layout of the template concurrently. Select View > Head Content (Ctrl+Shift+H/Cmd+Shift+H) so that you can see the head block content visually.

3 Position your cursor in line 17 (Meta Author tag) in Code view and select Modify > Templates > Make Attribute Editable. In the Editable Tag Attributes dialog that opens, set the following, then click OK:

   Attribute: CONTENT

   Make Attribute Editable: Checked

   Label: Meta_Author

   Type: Text

   Default Value: Enter Your Name Here!

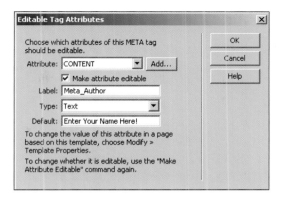

4 Position your cursor at the end of line 27 and type the following (or use snippet **MX Magic 2004 > Project 04 > 01-Comment_Mod_ Date Param**):

Listing 4.1

```
<!-- TemplateParam name="Comment_Mod_Date"
➥type="text" value="Month DD, YYYY" -->
```

Note: Once a child page is created, you can use the Contribute menu selection Format > Template Properties to modify these parameter values to the desired content. This is the only way to modify the value of `<meta>` tags within Contribute to be unique on each page.

You can repeat the process of step 3, using different values with the other `<meta>` tags that you wish to make editable within Contribute.

Keywords and Description can be handled without the use of parameters by adding these `<meta>` tags to the Editable Region named head. This won't meet your needs, however, because the site is already developed, and changes to Editable Regions of the Template file will not propagate to existing child pages. What you need to do is insert the `<meta>` tags in the locked region (to avoid this propagation issue) and set them up to use template parameters similar to step 3.

5   Scroll up to the Editor's Comments block (line 6) and replace the date value—July 20, 2003—with @@(Comment_Mod_Date)@@ (or use the snippet **02-Comment_Mod_Date Expr**). On line 7, replace the text Brad Halstead with @@(Meta_Author)@@ (or use the snippet **03-Meta_Author Expr**).

6   In Code view, position your cursor at the beginning of line 18. Insert two <meta> tags using Insert > HTML > Head Tags twice. Choose Description and then Keywords. For the value of each, type Add Content Here!.

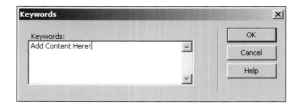

7   Position your cursor in the meta description tag and select Modify > Templates > Make Attribute Editable. In the Editable Tag Attributes dialog, set the following, and then click OK.

Attribute: CONTENT

Make Attribute Editable: Checked

Label: Meta_Description

Type: Text

Default Value: Add Content Here!

Note: Configuring the description and keywords this way enables the user to do everything from one interface instead of having them make various menu selections. It also saves you from having to perform a search and replace to put the meta tags in the Editable Region on all existing pages so that their values can be manipulated.

8   Repeat step 7 for the meta keywords on line 19, using a label of Meta_Keywords.

9   Select Modify > Templates > Check Template Syntax and click OK in response to the message. This verifies that the template markup written to the page is syntactically correct. If you see an error message here, then please review the previous steps for any mistakes you may have made.

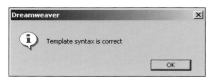

10   Save the modified template (Ctrl+S/Cmd+S). When the Update Template Files dialog opens, click the Update button. The Update Page dialog will show you which child pages were updated.

11   Click the Close button to close the dialog.

Modifying the Submenu System

It's been pretty straightforward thus far, but now you'll be converting the submenu system by employing a series of template elements to allow Contribute usability while maintaining your client's desire for accessibility enhancement. The Template elements used in this section will be an Editable Repeating Region, complex expressions manipulating the Expression Conditional Operator, and leveraging expression variables including _index and _isLast to your advantage.

Investigation

First, you must inspect the existing preliminary submenu system to see if there is any pattern that you can employ in the conversion process. Looking at line 35 (`<div id="SubNavLyr">`), notice the following:

Listing 4.2

```
<a href="page1.htm" tabindex="7" title="Product 2,
➡Page 1" accesskey="1">About Product 2</a>
➡<span class="hide"> | </span>
➡<span class="BreadCrumb">Product 2 FAQ</span>
➡<span class="hide"> | </span>
➡<a href="page3.htm" tabindex="9"
➡title="Product 2, Page 3"
➡accesskey="3">Product 2 Demo</a>
```

There is a link, a separator, a marker, a separator, and another link. The separator is only between the links and marker and is not repeated at the end of the link list. The marker has no link and has a class named BreadCrumb applied.

Table 4.1 Submenu System Patterns

	First Item	**Second Item**	**Third Item**
href	page1.htm	page2.htm *(Assumed)*	page3.htm
tabindex	7	8 *(Assumed)*	9
title	Product 2, Page 1	Product 2, Page 2 *(Assumed)*	Product 2, Page 3
accesskey	1	2 *(Assumed)*	3
link text	About Product 2	Product 2 FAQ	Product 2 Demo
class	N/A	BreadCrumb	N/A

There are several patterns that appear in the submenu system:

- **href:** Each page name is incremented by 1.
- **tabindex:** Each value is incremented by one and starts at 7.
- **title:** Each value has repeating content and the page value increments by 1.
- **accesskey:** Each value increments by 1.
- **link text:** There is a pattern but this needs to be editable, so the pattern will be abandoned.
- **class:** There is no pattern.

Conversion

Now that the patterns are outlined, you'll need to implement a method of using them to your advantage.

1   Position your cursor at the end of line 29 using Code view. Select the **04–PageNumber Param** snippet, and click the Snippet panel's Insert button to insert the following code:

Listing 4.3

```
<!-- TemplateParam name="PageNumber"
➥type="number" value="0" -->
```

This inserts a number type template parameter named PageNumber that will be used in expressions to evaluate which page you are currently on. The expressions will determine if a link is required for the sub-menu element or if it should be spanned with a breadcrumb CSS class with no hyperlink (the breadcrumb marker). There is no other reasonable method of adding this parameter to the template that doesn't require removal of some additionally modified element.

2   Position your cursor at the end of line 29 using Code view. Select the **08–SubLinkTitle Param** snippet, and click the Snippet panel's Insert button to insert the following code:

Listing 4.4

```
<!-- TemplateParam name="Access_SubLinkTitle"
➥type="text" value="Product #" -->
```

This inserts a text type template parameter named Access_SubLinkTitle that will be used to partially write the Accessibility attribute title for each link. There is no other reasonable method for adding this parameter to the template that doesn't require removal of some additionally modified element.

3   Find line 35, which looks like the following code:

Listing 4.5

```
<div id="SubNavLyr"><p><a href="page1.htm" tabindex="7"
➥title="Product 2, Page 1" accesskey="1">About Product 2</a>
➥<span class="hide"> | </span>
➥<span class="BreadCrumb">Product 2 FAQ</span>
➥<span class="hide"> | </span>
➥<a href="page3.htm" tabindex="9"
➥title="Product 2,Page 3" accesskey="3">
➥Product 2 Demo</a></p></div>
```

4   Replace line 35 with snippet **07–Line 35 Code**, which reads as follows:

Listing 4.6

```
<div id="SubNavLyr"><p><!-- TemplateBeginRepeat
➥name="RR_SubNav" -->
➥@@((PageNumber==(_index+1))?'<span class="BreadCrumb">':
➥'<a href="page '+(_index+1)+'.htm" tabindex="'+(_index+8)+
➥'"title="'+(Access_SubLinkTitle)+', Page '+(_index+1)+
➥'"accesskey="'+(_index+1)+'">')@@<!-- TemplateBeginEditable
➥name="ER_SubNav" -->About Product 2<!--
➥TemplateEndEditable -->
➥@@((PageNumber==(_index+1))?'</span>':'</a>')@@@@
➥ (!_isLast?'<span class="hide"> | </span>':'')
➥@@<!-- TemplateEndRepeat --></p></div>
```

5   Examine the changes you've made, reading from left to right across the line.

You have made the submenu content into a Template Repeatable Region called RR_SubNav that will allow you to create one or more of the submenu navigation elements. As you add repeats of this to the page, the number of repeats is contained in the _index parameter's value (counting from zero, of course) on the child page.

For each submenu element, the `PageNumber` parameter's value is compared to the `RepeatRegion`'s index value (`_index+1`). When they are the same, that submenu element is not assigned a link (this would be a redundant link to the page itself) and is only styled and acts as a breadcrumb marker. When they are different, that submenu element is assigned a link, which is styled by virtue of the pseudo-class definition.

The link that is assigned to the submenu element is also determined by the value of the `_index` parameter (as indicated in Table 4.1) by appending the parameter's value to the page name to produce page1.htm, page2.htm, page3.htm, and so on (`<a href="page'+(_Index+1)+'.htm`).

In addition, this link (when it is made) is also given a `tabindex` value, a `title` value, and an `accesskey` value (all of which are based on some variant of the `_index` parameter's value and the `Access_SubLinkTitle` parameter's value).

When these values are written to the child page, the first template expression in line 35 will have been evaluated (from the first @@ through the second @@).

When the `PageNumber` parameter and the `RepeatRegion` index are the *same*, the submenu element is styled with an opening `<span>` tag. When they are not the same, an anchor tag is opened with a pagelink. These opened tags must be properly closed. The next template expression does that by repeating the test. If it succeeds, the closing `</span>` tag is written. If the test fails, the closing `</a>` tag is written.

A final template expression is required to determine whether another breadcrumb will be needed (`!_isLast`). If it is, then a submenu element separator is written in preparation for the next repeated element. If it is not, then a null string is written, and the expression ends.

6 Select Modify > Template Properties > Check Template Syntax to verify that the existing template markup is syntactically correct. If it fails, go back and check your markup from step 3.

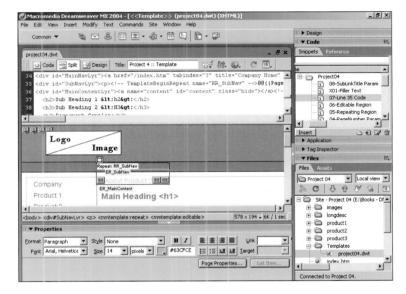

7 Save the template. A dialog might open stating that there is a potential issue with your newly inserted Editable Region. In this instance, you don't want the user to be able to add paragraphs to the submenu system, so it's okay to ignore this cautionary message and click OK to close it.

Validating the Template

You should know that Dreamweaver MX Template markup will fail validation especially when using template expressions. So what do you do to validate the template for Accessibility, XHTML, and CSS? Follow these steps:

1   Create a new page from the template (this is often referred to as *creating an instance page or child page*) using File > New > Templates Tab: choose Site "Project 04" and Template project04. Make sure to have a check in the Update Page When Template Changes check box or the generated page will not be a template instance and will not update when the template changes. Click the Create button to create the page and close the dialog.

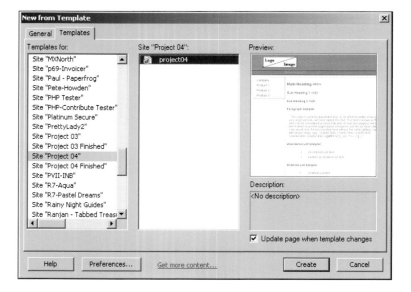

2   Immediately save the page in the root folder of the site, leaving it as `Untitled-x.htm`, where "x" may be any digit depending on your use of Dreamweaver MX 2004 this session. This properly updates paths to links, images, and attached stylesheets.

3   Add two repeating region entries by selecting the Repeating Region MUI + button twice.

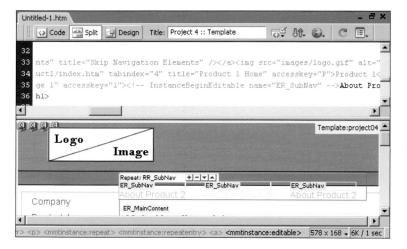

4   Choose Modify > Template Properties and change the parameter values to:

Access_SubLinkTitle: <u>Test Page</u>

Comment_Mod_Date: [*use today's date*]

Meta_Author: [*use your name*]

Meta_Description: <u>Sample Description</u>

Meta_Keywords: <u>sample,keywords</u>

PageNumber: <u>2</u>

Click the OK button to affect the change and close the dialog.

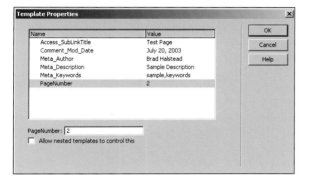

5   Save the page, and preview it by pressing F12.

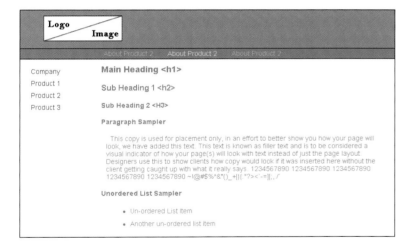

6   Upload the page and the site assets to your server and validate the URL by pointing your browser to the domain.

7   Once you're satisfied with the validation results (the child pages should validate fine with some manual checks required by Bobby), you're all done. Take this opportunity to see what the pages will look like with an over state and a normally linked submenu item in your browser.

8   Hand off what you've created to the client—with some minor instructions that are covered in the next section.

Creating the Site Pages in Contribute

What does the client need to know about creating child pages from this template in Contribute? This section will discuss the steps for creating new pages using this template.

Should the client need to create a new page, the steps are:

1   Select File > New Page, select the template from the appropriate connection (if more than one), provide a title value in the New Page dialog, and click OK to create the draft.

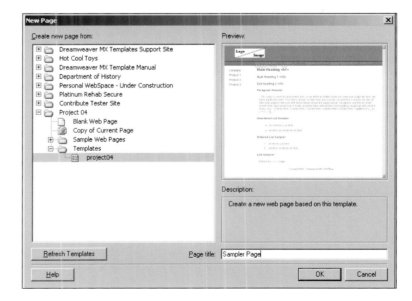

2   Select Format > Template Properties to set the template parameter values. (See the previous section "Parameter Information.")

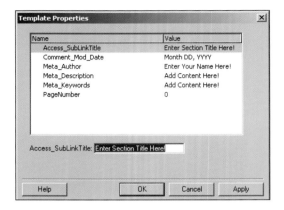

3   Add your submenu elements and main content, and publish the page.

Note: It's best to create the submenu system in the very first page, save that page, and then build pages using that page as a template. Contribute and Dreamweaver make you add each repeating element for each unique page; there is no other way of adding multiple inserted repeating regions.

Possible Pitfalls

As with anything you learn, there are advantages and disadvantages. You've learned all the advantages throughout this project but haven't heard many of the disadvantages.

- If you delete a menu item from a sectional group, you have to update the entire group of pages, including the index page. This will also require you to open now redundant files and save them with the required filename.
- If you add or delete a menu item from a sectional group, you have to update the entire group of pages, including the index page, as well as create the required document for the menu addition.

In my mind, the only true way to overcome these limitations is to use a server-side technology and employ an administration area that the client can use to update links and content.

Now Try This

By now you've learned how to use Dreamweaver templates and template elements to control meta data tags; convert an existing disjointed submenu system that stays compliant with current specs to control aspects of the submenu elements; validate the template for Accessibility, XHTML, and CSS; and create the site pages with Contribute by using the proper method of creating a new page from the template.

Here are some ideas on how to apply the skills you've learned or use the project you've completed in other ways:

- Limit the Contribute and Dreamweaver editor to five submenu elements. Once exceeded, display a warning message in a layer without using JavaScript! Hint: This should only require the addition of an optional region, one expression, one layer with its content, and a small addition to the CSS file!

- Using a template parameter, a template expression, and customized CSS files, change the colors of each sectional group of pages.

- Convert the main menu system from fixed to expandable, editable, accessible, and breadcrumb friendly. Hint: This should only require the addition of one parameter to the template and several expressions!

- Add an instructional layer to the page to show by default when the Contribute user is adding a new page. Hint: This should be an optional region.

Note: For additional methods of making a template navigational element a breadcrumb marker, read Project 3, "Managing Navigation Button States in Template-Controlled Sites."

If you need additional help with Dreamweaver MX templates, check out www.dwmagic.com/go/11 for more extensions and tutorials.

Integrating Dreamweaver and Fireworks in Your Projects

Kevin French

Kevin French is the founder and president of MM2K Inc., a full-service Internet company. He is also a self-taught Fireworks designer, a Team Macromedia Volunteer for Fireworks, and a Macromedia Dreamweaver Developer Certified Professional.

Fireworks has been my tool of choice for graphics creation, editing, and optimization since version 1 was introduced in 1998. Not only is it a great tool because of its powerful vector and bitmap handling, but because it also "plays well" with other applications like Dreamweaver.

The Fireworks/Dreamweaver integration is such a powerful and time-saving feature that is often overlooked. The synergistic relationship extends even beyond what I am able to share with you in this chapter. Fireworks MX 2004 enables you to check files in and out, FTP files to your server, and support roundtripping for server side-file formats. Additionally, from within the Dreamweaver MX 2004 environment, you can perform such Fireworks features as image optimization, cropping, resampling, sharpening, adjusting contrast and brightness, and even creating new images from image placeholders as you will learn in this chapter.

Please take some time to explore the powerful and time-saving integration between Fireworks MX 2004 and Dreamweaver MX 2004. I am sure you will be surprised at how your workflow will benefit from the harmonious relationship between these two great applications.

It Works Like This

Integration between Dreamweaver and Fireworks is a subject that everyone has heard of but few have fully explored. You'll use the creation of a simple brochure site of American landmarks to lead you down the less-traveled paths of Dreamweaver-Fireworks integration. Here are the basic steps of the project:

1 Save time and reduce your amount of work by setting up Dreamweaver's Launch and Edit in Fireworks feature.

2 Create Fireworks color palettes for one-click access in Dreamweaver with the help of the Harmonia Extension.

3 Use Dreamweaver Image Placeholders to design a web page layout before ever creating one image.

4 Convert Dreamweaver Image Placeholders to automatically create new images in Fireworks, simply by clicking one button.

5 Create Dreamweaver Library Items within Fireworks by exporting your file as an .lbi file.

6 Edit image Library Items in Dreamweaver.

You can use Image Placeholders to design a web page layout before ever creating one image.

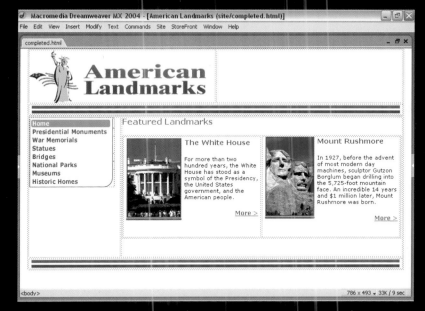

Here's the final web page with all the links in place.

Preparing to Work

Obviously, you are going to need both Fireworks MX 2004 and Dreamweaver MX 2004 to complete this project. If you do not have either of these applications, you can install the free trials located in the **Software** folder on the accompanying CD.

To prepare for this project, you will need to do the following:

1   Copy the **Projects/05/Site** folder from the accompanying CD to your computer.

2   Define a new site in Dreamweaver using the **05/Site** folder as your local root folder.

3   Install the Fireworks Harmonia extension, **Harmonia.1.0.0.mxp**, in the **Extensions** folder for Project 5. The Harmonia extension was developed by Kleanthis Economou of Project Fireworks (www.projectfireworks.com). See Appendix A, "Installing Extensions," for instructions on installing it.

Note: There is a strong possibility that the following steps were already configured automatically when you installed Dreamweaver MX 2004 and Fireworks MX 2004; however, you will not know this without following the steps. So, take a moment to make sure everything is exactly how you need it. The setup process will take less than a minute and has the ability to save you a considerable amount of time while working on your projects.

---

4   To achieve maximum integration between Dreamweaver MX 2004 and Fireworks MX 2004, you need to make sure that they are config-ured to "talk" to each other:

  • Choose Edit > Preferences or Dreamweaver > Preferences on the Mac.

  • In the Category column, choose File Types/Editors and select .png from the Extensions window. In the Editors window, make sure Fireworks (Primary) is listed.

  • If Fireworks is not listed, click on the (+) Add button above the Editors field, browse to the Fireworks MX 2004 executable, and click Open.

  • Click OK to confirm your choices.

  • Repeat these steps for the .gif and .jpg file types in the Extensions window.

Setting Up Dreamweaver's Launch and Edit in Fireworks Feature

You instruct Fireworks how to work with your source files (.png) when you choose to edit your files from within Dreamweaver. Being able to do this can reduce what is usually a long multi-step process that can be reduced to a few simple clicks.

1   In Fireworks, choose Edit > Preferences.

2   In the Launch and Edit tab, set When Editing from External Application and When Optimizing from External Application to Ask When Launching.

3   Click OK.

4   Save your work.

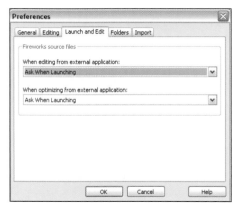

Creating Fireworks Color Palettes for One-Click Access in Dreamweaver

Before I design and build any site, I always think it's a good idea to define my color scheme. For this project, I decided to base my color scheme around the reddish color that is located in the **statue_liberty.gif** file that is part of the American Landmarks logo.

If you're like me, you may find it difficult to choose a harmonious color scheme when you are designing a logo or building a site. That tedious task of guessing which colors look best together is about to get much easier, thanks to a great Fireworks extension called Harmonia that automatically generates harmonious color schemes for you.

Color Schemes Defined

- **Complementary**: Made of two colors opposite each other on the color wheel. This combination gives high contrast, by using a warm color with a cool color.
- **Split-Complementary**: A variation of the complementary scheme that uses three colors. It uses a color, plus the colors that are on either side of the original color's complement. With this scheme you get an emphasis color, and two other colors that contrast and complement it.
- **Triadic:** Made of three colors that are equally spaced on the color wheel. This scheme produces a vibrant, balanced work by using warm and cool colors.
- **Analogous:** Composed of three "neighbor" colors, positioned next to each on the color wheel. One color dominates, while the other two enrich the composition.

---

1   Create a new Fireworks file that is 140 pixels wide and 40 high.

2   Select the Rectangle tool from the Tools panel, and draw three 40×40 pixel squares side by side. The Fill and Stroke colors do not matter.

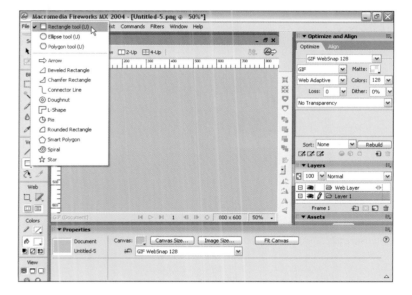

Tip: Holding the Shift key while using the Rectangle tool will ensure that the dimensions of the rectangles are perfectly squared.

---

3   Select the first square, and go to Commands > Project Fireworks > Harmonia.

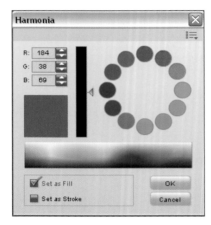

4   Enter the values R: 184, G: 38, and B: 69 into Harmonia. This is the same shade of red that is found in the American Flag of the **statue_liberty.gif** file.

Note: The color that represents the RGB values you just entered will appear in the 12 o'clock position of the Harmonia colorwheel.

---

5   Make sure Set as Fill is checked, and click OK.

6   Select the second square, and launch Harmonia again.

7   You are going to use a Triadic color scheme. The main color is in the 12 o'clock position, so count four colors clockwise to the 4 o'clock position, select it, and click OK.

Note: Remember, the rule of the Triadic color scheme says that your three colors are equally spaced on the color wheel.

---

8   Select your third square, and launch Harmonia again. The last color you selected is now in the main (12 o'clock) position.

9   Count four circles clockwise (to the 4 o'clock position), and select that color. Make sure Set as Fill is checked, and click OK.

10 Open the Optimize panel (F6). Set the Export File Format to GIF and the Indexed Palette to Exact.

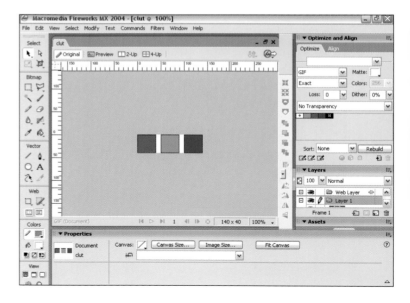

11   Save your Fireworks file as CLUT.png. Export the file to the Images folder within the site as **CLUT.gif** (**05/site/assets/images**).

Tip: *CLUT* stands for *Color Look-Up Table*. You will be using this file as a pseudo-color palette in Dreamweaver to ensure consistency with our color scheme throughout your project.

---

12   To access your new custom color palette in Dreamweaver, open the Assets panel (F11). Click on the Images icon in the upper-left corner. Select the CLUT.gif in the file list and a preview of your file will appear in the top window of the Assets panel. Click on the Add to Favorites button at the bottom of the Assets panel.

Note: Make sure that the Site radio button is selected.

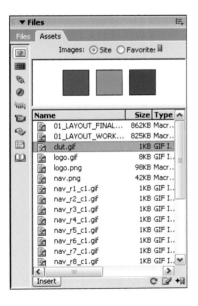

13   Select the Favorites button at the top of the Assets panel. Your custom color palette will now appear in the Favorites display window. You can select colors from this image with any of Dreamweaver's color pickers.

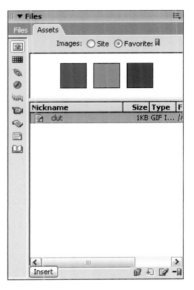

Using Dreamweaver Image Placeholders to Design a Web Page Layout

Image Placeholders are real time-savers when prototyping your web pages. They are temporary graphics that you can insert into your Dreamweaver documents during the design process. Essentially, they help you achieve a visually balanced layout between text and graphics before you even spend one second creating an image from within Fireworks.

Note: In Code view, you will notice that an Image Placeholder is nothing more than an `<img>` tag containing an empty src attribute. As with all `<img>` tags, the Image Placeholder's attributes can be customized by using the Attributes panel.

Try adding an Image Placeholder to the project page:

1   Open the **index.html** file in Dreamweaver (**05/Site/index.html**).

2   Place the insertion point in the cell that says `Insert Image Placeholder Here`, and choose Insert > Image Objects > Image Placeholder. (After inserting the Image Placeholder, delete the text that reads `Insert Image Placeholder Here`.)

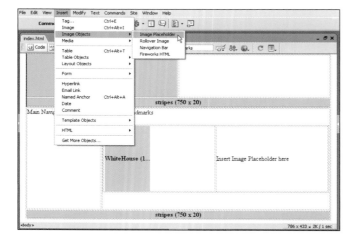

3   Set the following for the Image Placeholder:

   Name: <u>Rushmore</u>

   Width: <u>112</u>

   Height: <u>168</u>

   Color: Leave this blank

   Alternate Text: <u>Mount Rushmore</u>

Image Placeholder names can contain only letters and numbers (no spaces allowed) and cannot begin with a number.

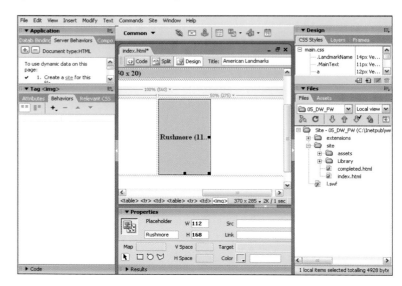

4   Click OK, and save your work.

Note: When viewed in the browser, the name and dimensions of the Image Placeholder will not appear as they do in the Dreamweaver environment.

Converting Dreamweaver Image Placeholders to Images in Fireworks

You can select any Image Placeholder in Dreamweaver and launch Fireworks to automatically create a new image. Fireworks will use the following Image Placeholder attributes in the creation of your new image:

- Image Placeholder Height and Width will translate to the Fireworks document canvas size.
- Image Placeholder Name will be used by Fireworks as the name of the source file and the exported file.

CAUTION

You may have noticed that certain properties in the Property inspector that are available for regular images are not available for Image Placeholders. This includes Image Alignment, Vspace, Hspace, Border, and Maps. These settings are not available because Fireworks does not recognize them. If you apply these properties to an Image Placeholder, they will be lost when you create an image from the Image Placeholder.

To try a conversion, start by creating the image that will replace the stripes Image Placeholder:

1   Select the stripes Image Placeholder, and click the Create button in the Property inspector. Dreamweaver will now launch Fireworks and create a new document with the dimensions of your Image Placeholder.

2   Using the Rectangle tool, draw a rectangle with the following properties:

    W: <u>740</u>

    H: <u>6</u>

    X: <u>5</u>

    Y: <u>2</u>

    Stroke: None

    Fill: <u>Solid, #B82645</u>

3   Duplicate the rectangle (Ctrl+Alt+D/Cmd+Opt+D) and apply these properties:

    W: <u>740</u>

    H: <u>6</u>

    X: <u>5</u>

    Y: <u>12</u>

    Stroke: None

    Fill: <u>Solid, #2645B8</u>

4   Click Done in the upper-left corner of the document window.

5   Fireworks will ask where you want to save your source file. Save the source file in 05/Site/assets/FW/.

Note: You will be prompted to overwrite the existing stripes.png file. Click OK.

---

6   Fireworks will ask where to export your bitmap version of the file. Browse to 05/Site/assets/images/ and click Save.

Note: You will be prompted to overwrite the existing stripes.gif file. Click OK.

Fireworks will automatically minimize, and Dreamweaver will be brought into focus. The stripes Image Placeholder has been replaced with the new image that you just created.

7   Now that you have created images from Image Placeholders, you're ready to replace Image Placeholders with existing images. Select the logo Image Placeholder.

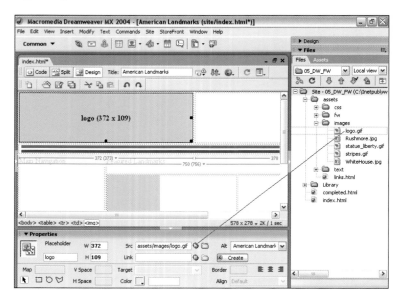

8   In the Property inspector, click on the folder icon next to the Src field. Choose the **logo.gif** file (**05/Site/assets/images/logo.gif**), and click OK.

9   Repeat steps 7 and 8 for the remaining Image Placeholders: WhiteHouse and Rushmore.

Note: After you replace the Image Placeholders for WhiteHouse and Rushmore, use the Property inspector to set the Align attribute to Left.

---

10   Save your document.

Creating Dreamweaver Library Items Within Fireworks

A *Library Item* is a file that will be used on multiple pages of your site and, when updated, will automatically update in every page in which it is applied. Navigation menus, company addresses, and graphics that are intended to be used extensively throughout a site design are all good candidates for exporting as Library Items. Library Items can be created from within Dreamweaver or from within Fireworks.

The creation of a Fireworks file that is going to be exported as a Dreamweaver Library Item is similar to creating any other file, with one exception.

All Dreamweaver Library Items must be located in a folder called Library, located in your site's root directory. This means that if your Library Item has root relative links, they should be prefaced with ../. This instructs the server to go up one directory before a link is executed.

For example, if you have a Library Item with a link to your home page as index.html, this link would actually look for a file named index.html within your Library folder. To reference your site's home page, your link should be formatted as ../index.html.

This link would go up one level from the Library folder to the root of your site and then look for your index.html file.

1 Open the **nav.png** file (**05/Site/assets/FW/nav.png**).

2 Select File and Export.

3 In the Export dialog box, select Dreamweaver Library (.lbi) from the drop-down in the Save as Type field.

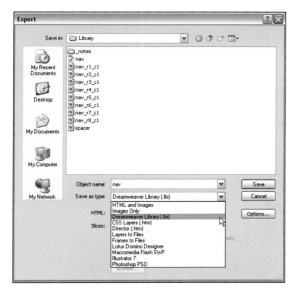

4 Click OK in response to this Alert window:

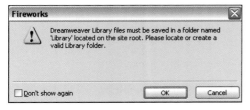

5 Select Export Slice in the Slices field.

6 Select the Library folder within the site's root that already exists.

7 When prompted to overwrite existing files, click OK. The nav.png file has now been exported to your site as a Library Item and is ready to be used.

8 Save your work.

Note: You also can create Text Library Items that can be used in Dreamweaver. Simply insert a slice into your Fireworks file, and from within the Property inspector, select HTML from the Type drop-down menu.

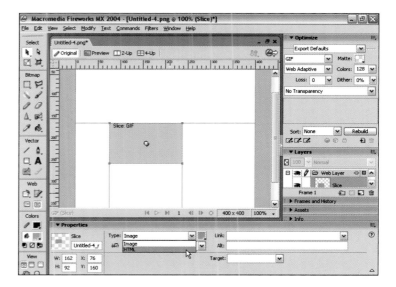

Click the Edit button on the Property inspector, and insert your HTML code:

```
<a href="http://www.yoursite.com">Your Site Link</a>
```

Fit the canvas to the size of your slice (Ctrl+Alt+F). Then, export the file as you would any Library Item, and it will be ready for use from within Dreamweaver.

Editing Image Library Items in Dreamweaver

As are all files created in Fireworks and exported to Dreamweaver, Library Items are fully editable from within Dreamweaver.

Try inserting the Navigation Library Item that you just created into your web page:

1   Open the Assets panel in Dreamweaver, and click on the Library icon, which is last icon on the left side of the Assets panel. A list of all of your Library Items will appear in the lower pane, and a preview of any selected Library file will appear in the upper pane.

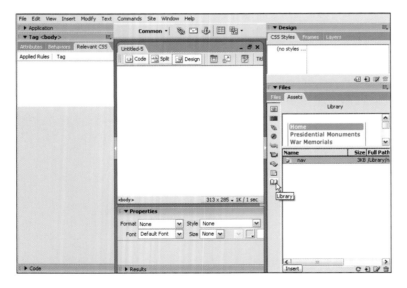

Tip: If the nav.lbi file does not appear in the Library, click on the Refresh button at the bottom of the Library panel to update your Library.

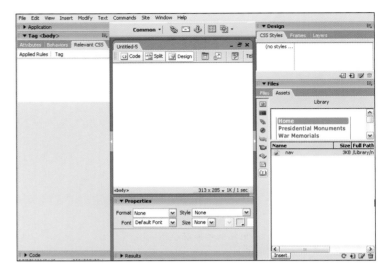

2   Select the nav.lbi file in the Library and drag it into your web page where it says `Main Navigation`.

3   Delete the Main Navigation text, and save the document.

Note: When you use a Library Item, Dreamweaver inserts a copy of the HTML source code for that item into the document, and adds an HTML comment containing a reference to the original Library Item.

Tip: When a Library Item is inserted into a Dreamweaver document, you will notice that it is highlighted. You can choose to turn this highlighting off or change the color of the highlight by going to Edit > Preferences > Highlighting.

4   There are several ways to edit a Library Item (see the following tip for five different ways to get your Library Item open). Once you've found one that works well for you, open the Library Item and select the part of the navigation that says Historic Homes.

Tip: There are several ways to begin the editing process of a Library Item from within Dreamweaver:

- Double-click the Library Item from within the Library in the Assets panel.

- Right-click the Library Item from within the Library in the Assets panel, and select Edit.

- Select the Library Item within the Library in the Assets panel, and click the Edit button at the bottom of the Library.

- Select the Library Item that is already inserted into your web page, right-click, and select Open Library Item.

- Select the Library Item that is already inserted into your web page, and click Open in the Property inspector.

---

5   In the Property inspector, change the alt field to read <u>Historic Homes</u>.

6   Save your .lbi file.

7   Dreamweaver will ask you if you want to update the Library Items used in the files in which they are referenced. Click Update, and then click Close in the Update Pages dialog. Any page that had a reference of the edited Library Item has been updated.

Tip: If your site contains multiple Library Items and you want to make sure that the page you are working in is referencing the most updated Library Items, select Modify > Library > Update Current Page.

---

8   At this point, all that is left to do to the page is to add your text and format it. You can find the text in **05/Site/assets/text/text.txt**. After your text is inserted, use the styles in the attached style sheet to format it. A completed version of the page is located at **05/Site/ completed.html**.

Now Try This

By now you've learned how to set up Dreamweaver's Launch and Edit in Fireworks feature, create Fireworks color palettes for one-click access in Dreamweaver, use Dreamweaver Image Placeholders to design a web page layout, convert Dreamweaver Image Placeholders to automatically create new images in Fireworks, create Dreamweaver Library Items within Fireworks, and edit image Library Items in Dreamweaver.

Here are some ideas on how to apply the skills you've learned or use the project you've completed in other ways:

- Now that you know how to use the Harmonia extension, you can drastically change the appearance of your page by using different color schemes. Because the project uses a Triadic color scheme, you should adhere to that. You can easily choose any other color that you may prefer, however, and base your new Triadic color scheme on that color.

- Try using the powerful Find and Replace feature in Fireworks and Dreamweaver to implement your new color scheme.

Translating a Fireworks Layout into a CSS + HTML Design

Kim Cavanaugh

Kim Cavanaugh has contributed numerous articles to Macromedia DevNet, has published two books on Dreamweaver and Fireworks and writes extensively for CommunityMX.com, covering the full range of Studio MX products. He is also a teacher for the School District of Palm Beach County (Florida) where he has been teaching middle school students web and graphic design using Dreamweaver, Fireworks, Freehand, and Flash since 1999.

There's an unmistakable buzz in the web development community over the use of Cascading Style Sheets (CSS) to replace many of the tried and true methods previously used for styling web pages. Out are font tags, nested tables, and the use of HTML attributes for styling page elements. In are the more efficient methods that CSS affords. The purists even go so far as to decry the use of tables of any sort to hold page structures together. Great! And just when I was getting good at that stuff!

Like many others, I'm a visual designer, and being required to work in a text editor to achieve a design has always been counterintuitive for me. For this project, I wanted to show how someone who likes to see his work unfold could bridge the world of visual design and CSS. My goal became how to illustrate the way a page could be designed in Fireworks and then have its visual aspects translated into a CSS design in Dreamweaver. The new tools that come built into Dreamweaver MX 2004 make this process much easier. I hope that once you see how a design can be put together with an eye toward maximizing your use of CSS, you too will be able to make the transition to the brave new world of CSS design.

It Works Like This

Designing page compositions in Fireworks is relatively easy. Combine the flexibility of Fireworks' vector drawing tools with the bitmap editing capabilities, and it's a simple task to build entire page designs in Fireworks. It's the next step that's always been the challenge. Here are the basic steps of the project:

1 Create a Fireworks composition that is easier to transfer to a lean HTML + CSS design by using multiple named layers.

2 Set the major properties for the page design by creating an external style sheet and modifying the `<body>` tag.

3 Create a simple page structure that uses a minimum number of tables and spacer images while remaining as true as possible to the original Fireworks concept.

4 Apply CSS styles to individual table cells using the new Tag inspector.

5 Control spacing and positioning of content in the page by assigning CSS selectors to individual areas of the design.

6 Modify the appearance of selected objects by creating and applying custom CSS classes.

7 Design navigation objects in CSS without the use of images by defining multiple link styles.

8 Insert and style an absolutely positioned `<div>` to complete the design.

Carefully constructing a design in Fireworks allows you to take full advantage of the lighter page weights, faster download times, and editing advantages found in CSS + HTML designs.

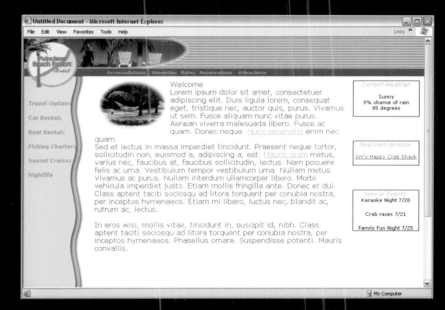

The final design of this web page features a heavy dose of CSS and minimum spacer images and nested tables found in more traditional page designs.

Preparing to Work

You are going to need both Fireworks MX 2004 and Dreamweaver MX 2004 to complete this project. If you do not have either of these applications, you can install the free trials located in the **Software** folder on the accompanying CD-ROM.

To prepare for this project, you will need to do the following:

1   Copy the files for this chapter from **Projects/06** on the accompanying CD to your hard drive.

2   Define a new web site in Dreamweaver MX 2004 using the 06 folder as the site root and name it <u>Project 06</u>.

3   From the **assets** folder in your Project 06 web site, open **pbr_layout.png** in Fireworks. In the event you are prompted about missing fonts, be sure to click the Maintain Appearance button so that all the text objects remain intact.

4   Open the Layers panel and note how the Show/Hide Layer symbol (the eyeball icon) has been toggled off for all the layers except Layout. Examine the layout and the notes that have been added for the design concept.

5   Click the Show Layer icon next to the Functional areas layer. Once the original sketch was completed, this layer was added so the functions of the different page elements could be seen more easily.

6   Hide the Layout and Functional areas layers, and click the Show Layers icon next to the other layers in the document.

7   Open and examine the file called **pbr_layout_sliced.png**. Three slices have been created for this image with each slice named and an appropriate file type set: header_photo, header_bg, and page_bg. Note that the Logo layer has been hidden because the logo and the photo at the top of the page overlap and can't be sliced easily. Note also that because the header_bg and page_bg slices are repeating elements, only a portion of each of those images has been sliced.

8   Look at **pbr_layout_logo.png**. This is a duplicate of the other files, except that all of the layers except the logo layer have been hidden and a slice has been added to capture the logo graphic, with the file type set to GIF and the slice named pbr_logo.

9   Export the slices from the two files or simply move on to the next section. You'll find all of the images you need in the **images** subfolder of your **assets** folder for this project.

Getting the *<body>* into Shape

Having examined the design concept, you should now have a good idea of how the page elements need to be styled. In this section, you'll create an external style sheet and set the common page properties for the page by redefining the <body> tag with CSS.

1   In Dreamweaver, start a new page. Create a standard HTML page, and save it as <u>index.htm</u> in the root folder of your site.

2   Open the CSS Styles panel and click the New CSS Style button at the bottom of the panel.

3   In the New CSS Style dialog, set the Selector Type option to Tag and the Define In option to New Style Sheet file.

4   Use the drop-down field at the top of the New CSS Style dialog to set the tag to body and click OK.

5   In the Save Style Sheet As dialog, name the file pbr_style.css and save it into the root folder of the web site.

The familiar Dreamweaver interface for creating style sheets will appear after you have completed those steps. Examining the page elements from the source Fireworks design reveals that a common font is used throughout the page, the page is set without margins, and the repeating graphic is used as a page background.

6   In the Style Definition dialog, set the text style to Verdana, Arial, Helvetica, sans serif with a color of #666666. Leave the text size unspecified, and set Line Height to 1.1 ems.

Leaving the text size unspecified allows the viewer's browser setting to set the size as needed. For most people, that will be the equivalent of 12 pixels. Because the design calls for a little spacing between lines, you need the Line Height value of 1.1 ems. An em is a proportional value based on the size of a text element. This setting equates roughly to a line height of 110%.

7   Select the Background category, and click on the Browse button next to the Background image field. Locate the **page_bg.gif** file inside the **assets/images** folder and click OK to set it as the page background.

Set the Repeat property to repeat-y. Set the Background color to white (#ffffff). These parameters set up the page background that repeats down the left side of the page.

8   Click the Box category, and set the Top Margin property to 0. Be sure that the Same for All check box is selected. This removes the default page margins.

9   Click OK to close the dialog. Switch to the CSS file, which should now be open, and save the CSS file. Save your page and get ready to insert the structure for the page in the next section.

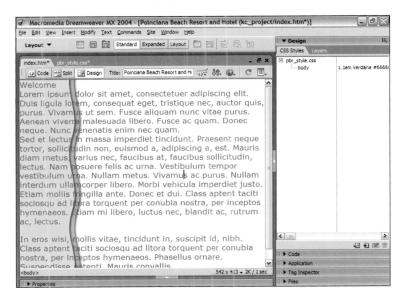

Note: In **Projects/06/assets**, you'll find **placeholder_text.txt**. Open it, and copy the text onto the page to see the effects that your new text style has on the page.

Styling the Tables with CSS

The functional areas of the design concept break the page into three regions: the header, the navigation bar, and the main content area. Because the design calls for a flexible page layout and you don't want to work with complicated positioning hacks required by lack of browser support, you'll insert three tables and apply the styling with CSS.

1   If you inserted the placeholder text previously, delete it now and be sure the cursor is at the top-left corner of the page.

2   Click the Table button in the Common category of the Insert bar, and insert a table with one row and four columns. Set the table width to 100% and set border thickness, cell padding, and cell spacing to 0. Make sure the Header option is set to None.

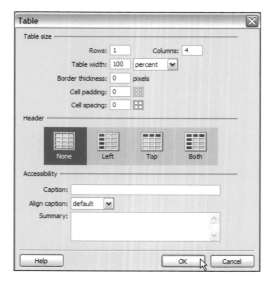

Note: While the `<table>` tag can be redefined using CSS so that all of the tables on the page are set to 100% width, the border and spacing CSS properties are not as faithfully rendered in all browsers (particularly older versions of Netscape). Setting standard HTML properties for the tables avoids that issue and also makes your design a bit easier to work with in Dreamweaver's Design view.

3   Click inside the upper-left table cell, and choose Insert > Image. Navigate to the file called **header_photo.jpg**, and insert it into the table.

4   Click the New CSS Style button in the CSS Styles panel, and set the Type to Advanced. Be sure the Define In setting displays the pbr_style.css file.

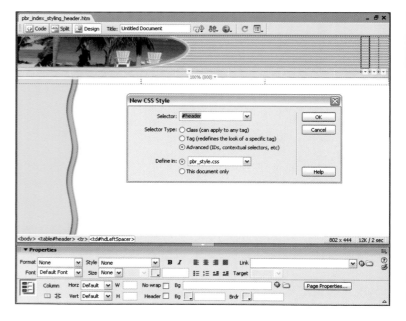

5   In the Selector field type in #header, and click OK. This style will be used to apply a background to the table you just inserted.

6   Choose the Background category—for the Background image property browse to the **header_bg.jpg** image in the **assets/images** folder—and click OK. Set the Repeat property to repeat-x, and click OK to close the CSS Definition dialog. This will be the only styling added to this table.

7   With the table selected, click the list menu for the Table ID in the Property inspector and choose header. Any unused ID selectors in your CSS file will show in this list menu.

Tip: Defining the style and then setting the ID using the Property inspector can help reduce spelling errors while setting up your styles, especially since styles are case-sensitive, and Dreamweaver doesn't honor casing in styles.

8   Next you'll style a table for the site navigation. Insert a new table below the header. It should have one row, seven columns with 100% width, and 0 borders, padding, and spacing.

9   Create a new style with the Selector Type set as Advanced, and type #mainNav into the Selector field.

10 In the Type category, set the color to #FFFFFF. Choose the Background category, and set a Background Color of #990099. Switch to the Block category, and set the Text align property to Center. Click OK.

As before, the Background property is set here. As you define new styles in an external style sheet, Dreamweaver will automatically open the CSS file. Right-click/Ctrl-click the tab at the top of the Document window and choose Save before previewing your work in a browser to ensure that your changes display properly.

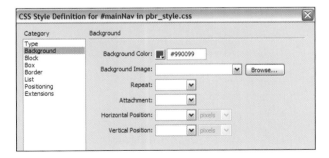

11 Select the new table you inserted, and choose mainNav for the Table ID in the Property inspector.

12 Insert a final table with one row and three columns below mainNav. Set border thickness, cell padding, and cell spacing to 0, and table width to 100%. Leave this table unnamed, but save your file.

Styling Individual Cell Properties with the Tag Inspector

One of the great new additions to Dreamweaver MX 2004 is the updated and revised Tag inspector. With this new and improved tool, applying IDs to individual page elements can be done entirely within the Dreamweaver workspace. For a visual designer, taking the next step of using CSS selectors to modify those objects just got a whole lot easier.

1   Click inside the header table to display Dreamweaver's new Table Selection tabs. Click the tab under the second cell from the left, and choose Select Column.

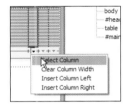

2   The first chore is setting the width of the cells in the header table. In the Tag inspector (F9), choose the Attributes tab to open that panel, and click the + next to the CSS/Accessibility category (if you're in Category view). In the ID field type in hdSpaceLeft.

To apply CSS selectors to individual table cells, you must give the cell an id.

3   Click the New CSS style button in the CSS Styles panel, and choose Advanced as the Selector Type. Type #hdSpaceLeft in the Selector field, and click OK to save the new settings into the pbr_styles.css file. Choose the Box category, and set the Width to 20 pixels.

This new style controls the width of the table cell, preventing it from collapsing. In the past, controlling cell widths would have been accomplished by inserting spacer images over and over again. Using selectors is a much more efficient way to accomplish the same task.

Note: I've borrowed a naming convention from Flash for applying the ids to individual objects on the page—starting with lowercase letters, and then uppercasing each new word in the filename. You can choose another method if you like, but remember that selectors cannot contain spaces or special characters, cannot start with numbers, and are case-sensitive. Choose a standard method for yourself, and stick to it.

---

4   Select the next cell to the right and give it an id of hdAdSpacer. Create a new style using #hdAdSpacer as the selector, and set the Width to 350 pixels. This cell sets space aside for an advertisement that may be added in the future.

5   Provide an id for the rightmost table cell of hdSpaceRight, and create a new style that sets the width of this cell to 20 pixels.

6   Move down to the mainNav table and select the leftmost table cell and give it an id of navSpaceLeft. Create a new style with the selector of #navSpaceLeft, and set the Width to 120 pixels in the Box category.

Here you're starting to apply spacing properties to the cells on the far right and far left of the mainNav table. This adds some control to the placement of the text links.

7   Tab to the next table cell in mainNav, and begin adding the text below, tabbing into the next cell as you complete each entry:

Accommodations

Amenities

Rates

Reservations

Attractions

This adds the text for the main navigation.

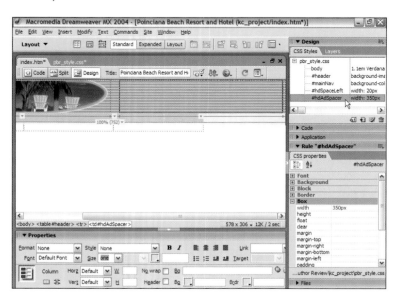

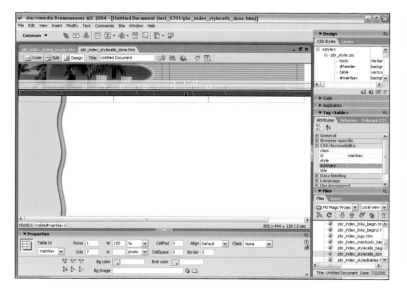

8   Select each word and type a pound sign into the Link field of the
    Property inspector to give the text a temporary link. You'll be coming
    back to the styling of the links in a bit, so don't worry about their
    appearance for now.

9   Select the rightmost cell, and give it an id of navSpaceRight. Add
    another new style, setting the Selector to #navSpaceRight, and apply
    a Width of 150 pixels in the Box category. This pushes things back
    together.

10 In the CSS Styles panel, select the #navSpaceLeft style that is listed and
    note how the applied styles are shown in the Relevant CSS Tab of the
    Tag inspector.

11 Save your page and the CSS file.

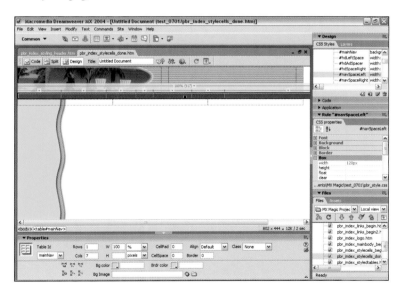

As you've added these new styles, each change has been recorded in the
style sheet. New in Dreamweaver MX 2004 is the ability to check and
change styles by using the Relevant CSS tab on the Tag inspector.

Styling Page Content with CSS Selectors

The main part of the page once again demonstrates the power of CSS and
gives you a good opportunity to see how simple styles can replace complex
tables with multiple spacer images. In this section, you'll apply the basic
properties required to match the conceptual design developed in
Fireworks. As before, the styling of this table will be accomplished by
modifying the individual cells.

1   Click inside the leftmost cell of the last table you inserted, and apply
    an id by choosing the Attributes tab of the Tag inspector. Name this
    cell mainLeft.

2   Add a new style, setting the Selector to #mainLeft. Follow the list in
    the table to set all the necessary properties into place. When you apply
    the padding values, be sure the Same for All check box is *not* selected,
    and then click OK.

Category	Property	Value
Block	Vertical Align	Top
Box	Width	130 pixels
Box	Padding—Top	55 pixels
Box	Padding—Right	10 pixels
Box	Padding—Left	10 pixels

3   Type in the following, pressing the Enter/Return key after each line and adding a pound sign in the Link field to create temporary links:

Travel Options   Fishing Charters

Car Rentals   Sunset Cruises

Boat Rentals   Nightlife

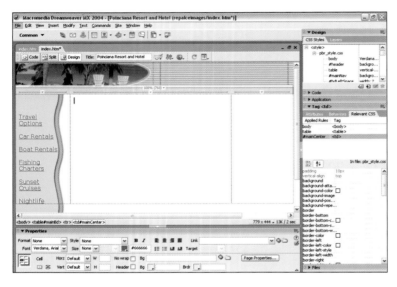

This adds the text for the secondary navigation.

4   Select the center table cell, and apply the id of <u>mainCenter</u>. Create a new style with the Selector set to <u>#mainCenter</u>, and set the Padding to <u>10</u> pixels in the Box category, with the Same for All check box selected. In the Block category set Vertical Align to Top.

5   Apply an id to the right cell of <u>mainRight</u>. Add a new style with the Selector set to <u>#mainRight</u>. In the Box category, set the width to <u>150</u> pixels and the Padding value to <u>10</u> pixels with the Same for All check box selected. Go to the Block category, and set the Vertical Align value to Top and Text Align to Center.

Note: As content is added into the Design view, you *should* see the design begin to take shape. If you notice small discrepancies in rendering in Dreamweaver, however, be sure to save the CSS file and check your design in a browser. While CSS rendering in Dreamweaver MX 2004 is better than previous versions, it's still not perfect.

6   In your Assets panel, locate the file called hammock.jpg and drag it into the center table cell of the page, called mainCenter. In the Property inspector, set the Align value for the image to Left. Press the right arrow key to move your cursor to the right of the image.

7   Open the **placeholder_text.txt** file, and paste its contents to the right of the picture or the hammock. As the text comes onto the page, it will be styled with the font type and size applied when the <body> tag was redefined.

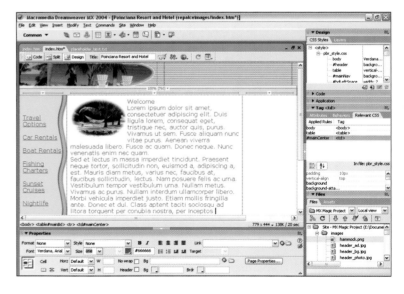

8   Add three new tables into the right column of the main table (mainRight). Set each with two rows and one column; set width to <u>100%</u> and padding, spacing, and border width to <u>0</u>. Insert a <p> tag between each table by pressing the Enter/Return key.

9   Start at the top, and add these three lines of text to each table in turn:

Current Weather

Featured Sponsor

Special Events

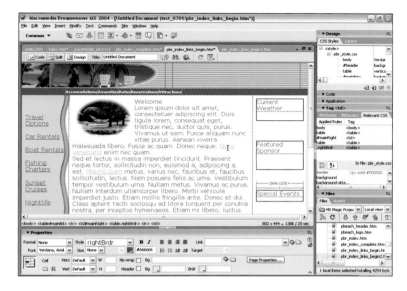

Each table needs its own text header, which you're adding here.

10   Save your files and preview your work in a browser.

Styling Individual Objects with Custom Classes

Up to now, you've been using CSS Selectors to style individual objects on the page. In this next section, you'll see how custom classes can be used to provide styling to elements on an as-needed basis. In particular, you'll be setting the styles that will be applied to the nested tables that you inserted in the last section.

1   Click the New CSS Style button, and choose Class. Make sure that the **pbr_style.css** file is still selected as the destination to save the new style. Name the style .rightHeader, and click OK.

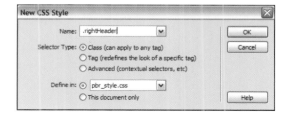

2   In the Style Definition dialog, choose the Type category and set Font Size to 0.8 ems. Set the color of the text to #FF9966, and the Style to Italic. Switch to the Block category, and set the Text Align property to Center. Click OK to close the Style Definition dialog and return to the page.

Note: You'll recall that 1em is equal in value to the size of the font element in use. Because this design calls for proportional spacing of fonts based on the viewer's settings, a value of 0.8em will show a font at 80% of its standard size.

---

3   To apply the new style, click on the text at the top of the right column (Current Weather), and then click the Style list in the Property inspector and choose rightHeader from the list. The style is added to the first block-level element that Dreamweaver finds—in this case, the `<td>` tag.

4   Repeat the process for the remaining table headings, using the same custom class for each. As you do so, the text will be transformed to match your Fireworks design.

5   Create a new style in the same manner, and set it as a custom class. Name the class .rightBody, and set the Type Size to 0.7em and the color to black (#000000).

6   Add some dummy text in the second row of the three tables. (Don't forget Karaoke night!) Assign the class to the three table cells as you did in step 5.

7   Save your work.

Styling Navigation Links

In this section you'll be using a different form of CSS Selector to define three link styles for the page: the default links, the main navigation links, and the links for the secondary navigation on the left side of the page.

1   Add a new CSS style and set the Selector Type to Advanced. Click the drop-down arrow, and choose a:link. Be sure that you are still work-ing in the **pbr_style.css** file.

2   Place your cursor in front of the a in the Selector field, and type in #mainNav. The selector will now read #mainNav a:link. Be sure that there is a space between the letters "v" and "a."

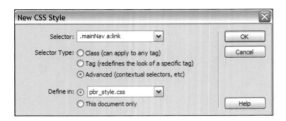

3   Click OK, and in the Style Definition dialog, set the Text Size to 10 pixels and the color to white (#FFFFFF). In the Decoration settings, check None and then click OK to close the first definition.

Unlike the previous text elements, the design calls for the navigation bar text to remain at the same size, and therefore a fixed pixel size has been chosen.

4   Add another new style using the CSS selector of a:visited. Type #mainNav in front of the selector. Use the same 10 pixel size, set the color to #CC99CC, and set Decoration to None. Remember that there needs to be a space between the class and the selector.

5   Create links for the a:hover and a:active selectors, type #mainNav ahead of them. Use a color of #FF9966 for hover and white (#FFFFFF) for active. Be sure that Decoration is None for both. This finishes the main navigation styling.

Tip: There's a well-known mnemonic device to help you remember that link styles must always be applied in a specific order. Link-Visited-Hover-Active; or LoVeHAte. If you can remember Love-Hate, your links will always be styled in the proper order.

If your text seems a little too insubstantial, you can always edit the style and change the Weight value in the Type category to Bold. You only need to edit the four styles to have the change take effect with all your links—the power of CSS!

6   Create two additional link styles to set your design into motion, one for the left navigation (#mainLeft a:[pseudo-class]) and one for the main links in the page (#mainCenter a:[pseudo-class]). Refer back to the original design concept in Fireworks to see how the sizes and colors of the links might be applied.

7   Save your work.

Inserting One Lone *<div>*

Remember the logo for the Resort? The one that just seemed too hard to place into the page design? That's the very last step you need to tackle, and this time you'll get the job done by creating an absolutely positioned <div> to handle the job.

1   Add a new style, set the Selector Type to Advanced, and name it #logo. Be sure you are still working in the **pbr_style.css** file.

    While it seems a little backwards, the first step in inserting the image is to define the container that it will go into in CSS.

2   Select the Positioning category and set Type to Absolute, Width to 121 pixels, Height to 127 pixels, Top to 0 pixels, and Left to 0 pixels. Click OK. The values used in defining the size and position of the logo <div> were obtained from the Property inspector in Fireworks.

3   Choose Insert > Layout Objects > Div Tag. In the Insert Div Tag dialog, set the ID value to logo, the Insert list to Before tag, and choose <table id="header"> from the last list.

This is another new feature of Dreamweaver MX 2004 that allows you to work with absolutely positioned <div> tags without having to remove the inline style that previous versions of Dreamweaver inserted into the page.

4   The placeholder text will already be selected, so just delete the text before you insert the logo.

5   With the cursor still inside the logo <div>, insert the file called **pbr_logo.gif** from your **images** folder.

6   Save the CSS file, and preview your work in a browser.

Now Try This

By now you've learned how to create a Fireworks composition that is easier to transfer to a lean HTML + CSS design, take advantage of the tools in Dreamweaver MX 2004 to make the process of easing into the world of CSS-based design less painful, and make the file weight for the sample page as small as possible while remaining as true as possible to the original Fireworks concept.

Here are some ideas on how to apply the skills you've learned or use the project you've completed in other ways:

• Go back into your style sheet and do some final tweaking to improve the design. Is the navigation bar spreading out too much? You can easily fix that by changing the Padding value in the navigation bar by locating the named element that controls that property. Want to change the text styles, border colors, or any of the styled elements on the page? It's a snap now that you know where they're defined and how to access the settings.

• Don't like the link styles? Again, now that you know how the properties have been applied, it's a much simpler matter to head directly to the CSS file to change the styling.

• Of course, as your CSS chops improve you may want to explore the brave new world of pages built entirely in CSS with no tables at all. It's entirely possible, and now that you have an appreciation for the elegance of CSS from a designer's viewpoint, it may well be a task that you're ready for.

PROJECT 7 | Using Flash in Dreamweaver

Edoardo Zubler is a
multimedia developer and
Macromedia Team
Volunteer who specializes
in creating rich media
applications for a wide range
of devices and platforms.

Edoardo Zubler

I'm definitively addicted to entertainment multimedia, and I remember how thrilled I was
back in the days when FutureSplash made its first appearance in MSN. Ever since then, I've
always been passionate about Macromedia Flash, and I've always used it on every multimedia
project I've done.

One of the benefits of using Dreamweaver for web development is that it offers you limitless
possibilities for integrating and managing Flash content on the web: from merely embedding
external Flash movies to generating on-the-fly Flash Objects and to using the brand-new
Flash Elements. This chapter, written from a Dreamweaver user's perspective, teaches you how
to get the most out of some of these methods, and shows you how you don't necessarily have
to be a Flash developer to enhance the user experience by adding rich media Flash content to
your projects.

It Works Like This

Just like its two predecessors, Dreamweaver MX 2004 comes with a full-featured set of ready-to-use Flash Objects: Flash Buttons and Flash Text. These are astounding timesavers when it comes to creating custom navigation bars. Here are the basic steps of the project:

1   Use Dreamweaver's built-in Flash Objects and additional external Flash assets to complete a web site for a fictional amusement water park named Hungry Shark.

2   Create a flashy navigation bar using Dreamweaver Flash Objects.

3   Embed external Flash movies inside an HTML page and send data to them using FlashVars.

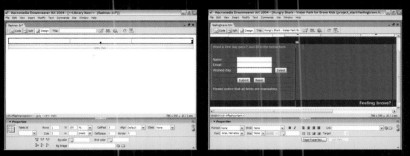

Use some of Dreamweaver's built-in Flash Objects to make your site even more spectacular.

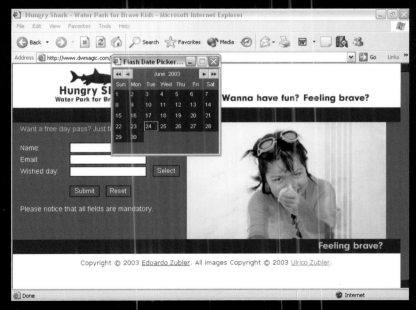

Here is the finished page, complete with a Flash Date Picker.

Preparing to Work

To prepare for this project, you will need to do the following:

1 Install the extension **flash_date_picker.mxp** from the **Projects/ 07/Extensions** folder on the CD. See Appendix A, "Installing Extensions," for more information.

2 Copy and paste the **Projects/07/project_start** folder from the CD to your hard drive.

3 Define a new site using the project_start copy as your site root.

4 Because this project mainly focuses on integrating Flash and Dreamweaver, most of the site structure has been created for you. A few items are still missing: a navigation bar common to all the pages, a date picker for the contact form that enables users to ask for a free daily pass to the park, and a few of those flashy effects that will excite visitors.

   To set up the missing elements, start creating the Library Item that contains the main Flash navigation bar. Choose File > New. From the Basic Page category, choose Library Item. The New Document dialog appears providing you with several choices.

5 Click the Create button. The New Document dialog closes, and you are provided with a new blank Library Item.

6 Switch to Show Code and Design views or Show Code view, and remove the <meta> tag at the top of the page.

7 Save the document as flashnav.lbi into the Library folder.

Note: With more than 40 Flash Buttons styles, Dreamweaver MX 2004 has everything you need to flash up your web pages in a snap. Nevertheless, if the buttons that ship with Dreamweaver MX 2004 are not to your taste or are not enough for you, you can look for additional sets on the Macromedia Exchange. To do this, simply click on the Get More Styles button in the Insert Flash Buttons dialog box. A new browser window will launch, displaying the Dreamweaver area of the Macromedia Exchange. Make sure you are searching the Dreamweaver Exchange, enter the phrase Flash+buttons as your search term, choose Flash Media as the Category, and then click the Search button.

Generator Is Dead. Long Live Generator.

Dreamweaver Flash Objects are created directly inside Dreamweaver thanks to an embedded version of a program called *Macromedia Generator*. If you've never heard of it, all you need to know is that Generator was a Java-based server technology created by Macromedia, which was able to generate Flash files on-the-fly by passing parameters to Flash Template files (SWT files).

With the release of Flash MX, Macromedia ceased further development of the Generator Server family and replaced it with a more feasible technology called *Macromedia Flash Remoting MX*, which better fit with Macromedia's new vision of Rich Internet Application (RIA). For the same reason, the Macromedia Generator Authoring Extension, which is required if you want to create your own custom sets of Dreamweaver Flash Buttons and Generator templates (SWT files), is only compatible with Flash 5 and doesn't install with any newer version of Flash.

This means that if you do not have an old copy of Flash 5, you can not create Generator-based Flash Buttons. However, with newer versions of Flash, you can still create Flash Buttons that replicate the functions of Generator-based buttons inside Dreamweaver in many other ways. One is the adoption of the FlashVars property of the Flash Player, which you will learn to use in this project. Take FlashBang! Buttons, for instance. These are a more flexible Dreamweaver Flash Buttons-like solution, which takes full advantage of FlashVars. Offered as an alternative to standard Macromedia Flash Buttons, FlashBang! buttons are available as a commercial Dreamweaver extension by Joseph Lowery and Edoardo Zubler at www.flashbangmedia.com.

Editing Library Items

Time to insert the HTML elements that will host the navigation bar driven by Flash Objects.

1   With your new Library Item still open, switch back to Design view.

2   Select Insert > Layout Objects > Div Tag. The Insert Div Tag dialog appears, letting you specify the CSS Class you want to attach to your `<div>` tag and the layer's ID. Because no CSS file has been linked to this document, both the Class and the ID list menus are empty.

3   Type <u>flashnavigation</u> into the ID field, and click the OK button.

Giving an ID to the layer helps you identify it as a distinct element of the page it is inserted into. In addition to this, because the CSS Style provided with this project contains an ID selector for flashnavigation, the layer ID eases the positioning of every instance of this Library Item throughout the site.

When you click OK, the `<div>` tag is inserted and a sentence saying `Content for id "flashnavigation" goes here` is added to the flashnav.lbi document.

Note: CSS ID selectors are used on a per-element basis and refer to the ID attribute in HTML code.

---

4   Delete the sentence `Content for id "flashnavigation" goes here`, and click on the Table button in the Common category of the Insert bar. The Insert Table dialog appears, offering twice the options it did in Dreamweaver MX, thanks to the addition of graphical elements that let you easily identify each part or attribute of the HTML table to be inserted into the document.

5   Enter the following values into the Insert Table dialog:

Rows: <u>1</u>

Columns: <u>3</u>

Table Width: <u>100%</u>

Border Thickness: <u>0</u>

Cell Padding: <u>3</u>

Cell Spacing: <u>0</u>

These settings create a simple, three-column table with a 3-pixel space between the cells' content and the cells' boundaries.

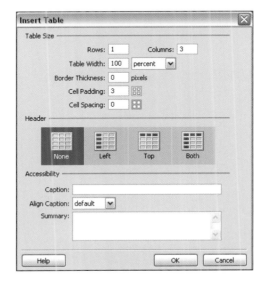

6   Click OK to insert the table.

7   Save your work.

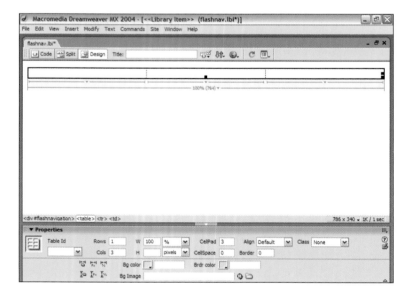

Using Dreamweaver Flash Text

Everything is now in place to add some Flash Objects to the main navigation bar. Because the design of this project's web site is quite clean, you will use basic Flash Text objects instead of more eye-catching Flash Buttons.

1   Click inside the first cell of the table and choose Insert > Media > Flash Text. The Insert Flash Text dialog appears.

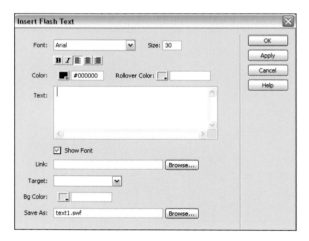

2   Choose your preferred font from the Font pop-up menu, and set the font size to 20.

Note: The font used for this project is Neuzeit Grotesk Black, created by Wilhelm C. Pischner and available for purchase at URW++ (www.urwpp.de), but you can use any sans serif font.

---

3   Complete the remaining fields using the following values:

   Color: #003366

   Rollover Color: #336699

   Text: Boring summer?

   Bg Color: #FFFFFF

4   Select the **index.htm** file as the Link using the Browse button near the Link field. You'll need to go up one level when the Select File dialog appears. This redirects the user to the index.htm document each time they click on the newly created Flash Text.

Note: Notice that site root-relative links are not accepted by Flash Objects, because browsers are unable to recognize them within the SWF files. When creating links from Flash Objects, always use absolute or relative paths only. Besides this, when using document-relative links, a good practice is to save the Flash files into the same directory as the HTML document that encloses them. Do this to avoid problems with different browser interpretations of document-relative links. Because you are using document-relative links within the SWF files of a Library Item in this project, I suggest you convert those links into absolute ones before deploying the site to a production server.

---

5   Enter boringsummer.swf as the name of the Flash movie in the Save As field, and click OK.

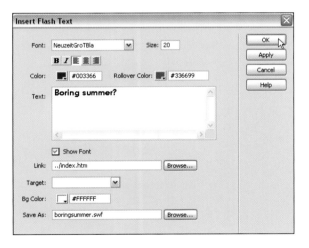

Note: In Design view, you can preview any media object you insert into your current document using one of two techniques. The first technique consists of selecting the media object placeholder and clicking on the Play button on the Property inspector. The second is choosing Plugins > Play (or Play All, depending on how many objects you wish to preview at the same time) from the View menu.

---

6   Repeat steps 2 through 5 to insert two additional Flash Text objects into the two remaining table cells. Use the following sets of values:

> Color: #003366
>
> Rollover Color: #336699
>
> Text: Wanna have fun?
>
> Link: ../fun.htm
>
> Bg Color: #FFFFFF
>
> Save as: fun.swf

> Color: #003366
>
> Rollover Color: #336699
>
> Text: Feeling brave?
>
> Link: ../feelingbrave.htm
>
> Bg Color: #FFFFFF
>
> Save as: feelingbrave.swf

Note: At any time, you can modify any of the Flash Text objects you just inserted. Simply double-click their placeholder or select the object and click on the Property inspector's Edit button. Either method will open the Insert Flash Text dialog for editing.

---

7   Save and close flashnav.lbi.

Inserting Library Item Instances into Documents

The Flash navigation bar is now ready to be inserted into the web site pages.

1   Open index.htm, and switch to Code and Design view or Code view.

2   Place the insertion point right before the `<div>` tag with an `id` of `textcontent`, which is located close to the opening `<body>` tag. Use Code and Design view to have a clear view of your document structure when you're adding new content.

3   Select the **flashnav** item from the Library category of the Assets panel, and click the Insert button to have the Flash navigation bar inserted into the page.

CAUTION

Once inserted into a document, Library Items are surrounded by special comment tags. It is important that you don't remove these tags, otherwise Dreamweaver will not be able to update the Library Item if you modify it. In addition to this, these tags are used by Dreamweaver to highlight the item with a bright yellow background color both in Design and Code views, helping you track every Library Item inserted into the document.

4   Repeat steps 1 to 3 for the **fun.htm** and **feelingbrave.htm** documents.

5   Save and close all your open documents.

Using *FlashVars*

Before going further with this project, take a second to preview the site in a browser. As you can see, both index.htm and fun.htm contain a picture on their right side. Rolling over those photos triggers a fancy effect scripted inside a Flash movie. These two pages use the same Flash movie, but differ by a couple of attributes set using `FlashVars`.

Now you are going to add this Flash movie to the feelingbrave.htm page, and define which picture to display using the `FlashVars` property of the Flash player.

Note: If you have ever worked with external Flash assets, you have probably been told that the easiest and fastest way to set variables inside a Flash movie is to append them on a query string right after the name of the Flash file in the HTML tags used to embed the file on the web page. This was true until the release of Flash Player 6, which introduced the `FlashVars` property. `FlashVars`, in a sense, is similar to the query string technique, because all the name=value pairs have to be URL encoded. It differs from that technique because all variables are created before the first frame of the SWF is played, making them immediately available to the Flash movie.

1   Open the **feelingbrave.htm** file in Design view.

2   Place your cursor inside the `<div>` tag with an `id` of `flashcontent` that is located on the right of the form, and select Insert > Media > Flash.

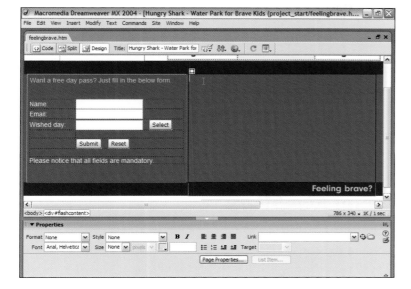

3   Browse to and select hs_imagefx.swf in the Select File dialog box and click OK. The SWF file is embedded into the document and the Property inspector changes its options to display the Flash movie properties.

Note: If you have Flash installed on your system, you can launch it to edit the source FLA file directly from Dreamweaver by simply clicking on the Edit button of the Property inspector. You can find the source FLA file of the Flash movie used in this project in the assets folder of your site.

---

4   Click on the Parameters button in the Property inspector. The Parameters dialog appears, letting you enter values for special parameters defined for the Flash movies. In this project, you use it to define the `FlashVars` property of the Flash Player.

Note: The Parameters dialog is not used just for Flash movies. It can be used with any media object, such as ActiveX, plug-ins, or Java applets.

---

5   Type <u>FlashVars</u> in the Parameter field, and type tmtImage=images/ hs_feelingbrave.jpg&tmtImageChrome=images/hs_feelingbrave Chrome.jpg in the Value field.

The effect on the Flash movie is achieved by simply combining two different images and a scripted mask. The values you just entered are nothing but the relative paths to the two images that need to be loaded inside the Flash movie.

6   Click OK to close the Parameters dialog box, and, making sure that the Flash movie placeholder is still selected, press the Property inspector's Play button to preview the effect. When you are satisfied with it, you can save your document.

Using the Flash Date Picker Extension

The Flash Date Picker helps users insert properly formatted dates into forms. All the variables needed by the Flash Date Picker are passed to it using FlashVars and a JavaScript function. Let's now put the extension to work.

1   In Design view, click the Select button on the form in the feelingbrave.htm document.

2   From the Behaviors panel (Shift+F3), click on the Add Behavior (the + sign) button and choose DWMagic > Flash Date Picker. The Flash Date Picker dialog appears.

3   Select text "date" in form "freepass" in layer "textcontent" from the Field pop-up menu to choose which field of the form the date should be inserted into.

4   Select MM/DD/YY as Date Format and Shark as Style for the Flash Date Picker, and then click OK.

Note: The Flash Date Picker comes with two predefined date format styles (US and European) and two different skins to choose from.

5   Save the feelingbrave.htm document and test the entire project in a browser.

Note: Always remember to save your document before inserting the Flash Date Picker behavior; otherwise, the behavior will not be available. It is grayed out because the extension is not able to determine where to save the SWF until the file you're adding the behavior to has been saved.

Note: Even though the Flash Date Picker can help prevent the insertion of a badly formatted date, adding some kind of validation to your forms is always good practice. An extremely useful extension, which makes accomplishing this task awfully easy, is Check Form MX by Jaro von Flocken, available as a free download from www.yaromat.com.

Now Try This

By now you've learned how to use Dreamweaver's built-in Flash Objects to complete a web site creating a flashy navigation bar using Dreamweaver Flash Text, and how to embed external Flash movies inside an HTML page and send data to them using FlashVars.

Here are some ideas on how to apply the skills you've learned or use the project you've completed in other ways:

• If you have Flash MX or Flash MX 2004 installed on your system, try to open and edit the source FLA file contained in the **assets** folder of this project to make it accept even more variables; then practice passing data to it using FlashVars.

• Once you're more confident using FlashVars, try using it to replace the Flash Text objects used for the main navigation bar with custom-made Flash movies.

Sending a Form to Email

Danilo Celic, Jr. is a partner at CommunityMX.com and a member of Team Macromedia. He frequently comes to the aid of budding extension developers in the Macromedia support forums.

Danilo Celic, Jr.

Ahhh, Las Vegas—city of so many sights and sounds that it strives for your attention, and strongly grasps to keep it. Despite the various distractions available to us, Massimo and I sat in his hotel room near the end of another fulfilling and quite tiring geekfest that is known as TODCON. While we worked on separate projects, we were talking about what would eventually become this book. "It's all about communication," I thought to myself as I considered the network that we were using to connect to the Internet, the applications we were writing, and in turn, the very conversation we were having.

Ideas, thoughts, instructions, and requests—the very lifeblood of communications online, and many of our conversations, are held via email. Then the topic of the conversation going on *outside* my head became "What would *I* consider a good topic for this project." Since email communication was on my mind, Massimo and I turned quickly to talking about a common use of email in web development: a form is submitted, and an email is spit out. I'd bet you that in Vegas still there are bells ringing, lights flashing, and coins clattering, but hopefully we can avoid the distractions for the duration of this project and facilitate a little communication through email.

It Works Like This

A major draw to Dreamweaver MX 2004 is its ability to easily produce server-side code. To many, this means databases, master-detail page sets, and writing SQL statements. There's more to server-side coding than just databases, however. One of the most common requests that clients have is to place a contact form on their site and have the entries of that form sent to an email address—frequently to their sales or customer service email address—so that someone within the company can respond to the visitor who filled out the form. Here are the basic steps of the project:

1   Use Dreamweaver's sample CSS style sheets to give your pages a styling jumpstart.

2   Create a ColdFusion, ASP VBScript, or PHP Contact Us page with a form on it using a table for layout.

3   Use Dreamweaver form objects to add text fields, radio buttons, a select menu, check boxes, a textarea, and buttons to your contact page form.

4   Build a Thank You page using the DWMagic Mailer Server Behavior that can process site visitors' form submissions on the Contact Us page, and then send an email containing those form entries.

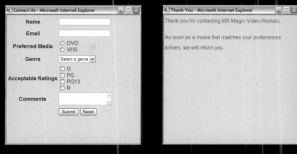

Set up the DWMagic Mailer Server Behavior to create a thank-you email.

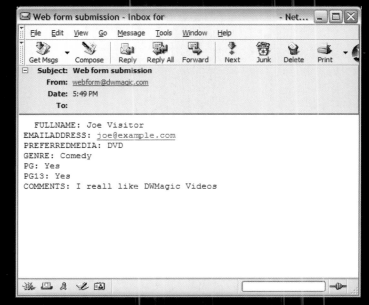

Here's the completed email.

Preparing to Work

To prepare for this project, you will need to do the following:

1   Install the **DWMagic Mailer.MXP** extension located on the CD in the **Projects/08/Extensions** folder. See Appendix A, "Installing Extensions," for instructions.

2   Create a site that has a server model set to any of the following: ColdFusion, ASP VBScript, or PHP.

3   Be sure to set appropriate information in the Testing Server category of the Site Definitions dialog to a hosting account where you have email capabilities so that you can upload your pages for testing when the project is completed. For an ASP VBScript site, the hosting account must have the CDONTS mailer component available for your use.

4   If you already have a site defined with a ColdFusion, ASP VBScript, or PHP MySQL server model that you'd like to use, then open that site and create the project's files within that site.

5   Optional: Copy the appropriate files for your server model from **Projects/08/finished** into your site to see examples of completed pages for each server model.

6   Prior to testing any of the pages in the finished folder, make sure that you make changes to the email addresses used in the example pages. Go to the "Editing an Existing Server Behavior" section near the end of this chapter for information on how to make changes.

7   In the Files panel, ensure that the site created in step 2 is the active site.

8   Create the Contact Us page by choosing File > New. On the General tab of the New Document dialog, select Dynamic Page in the Category field. Choose the type of dynamic page for your server model from the list on the right. Click Create.

For the duration of this project, we'll be using ColdFusion. You might want to follow along using ASP VBScript or PHP, using the appropriate file extensions (.asp and .php, respectively) in place of the ColdFusion file extension (.cfm).

9   If you are interested in creating XHTML pages, prior to clicking the Create button, check the box next to Make XHTML Compliant in the lower right of the New Document dialog.

10 Save the file as contact.cfm with your site.

11 Give contact.cfm a title of Contact Us in the Title field of the Document toolbar.

12 Repeat steps 8 through 10, titling the file Thank You and saving it as thankyou.cfm.

Adding Styling to Your Pages with CSS

To avoid "plain Jane" pages (and to learn a couple more features of Dreamweaver MX 2004), you're going to add some CSS to the two pages you just created.

1   Make contact.cfm the active document.

Note: A couple keyboard shortcuts help you navigate between document tabs. Ctrl+Tab/Cmd+` makes the tab to the right of the current tab active. If the current tab is the rightmost tab, then the first tab on the left becomes the active tab. Ctrl+Shift+Tab/Cmd+Shift+` performs the same operation, but moves to the left.

2   Open the CSS Styles panel, and click the Attach Style Sheet button to
    open the Attach External Style Sheet dialog.

3   On the lower left of the dialog, click the Sample Style Sheets link to
    open the Sample Style Sheets dialog.

4   Select Full Design: Accessible from the list of sample style sheets.

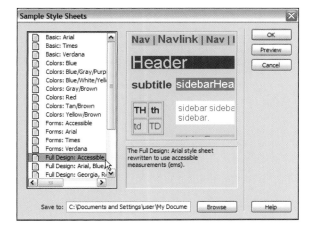

5   Click the Browse button, select a folder within your site to store the
    new style sheet, and then click OK to attach the newly created style
    sheet to your document.

Tip: If you have an existing page to which you'd like to attach one of
Dreamweaver MX 2004's sample style sheets, but you're not sure
which one would look best with your page, press the Preview button.
Your page behind the dialog will be displayed using the styles defined
in the selected sample style sheet. Don't worry—if you don't like the
effect, clicking the Cancel button will remove the styles displayed using
the Preview button.

6   Switch back to thankyou.cfm, and click the Attach Style Sheet button
    in the CSS Styles panel.

    Accessible_Design.css, the CSS file created in step 5, should be listed
    in the File/URL field of the Attach External Style Sheet dialog. If not,
    click Browse and find Accessible_Design.css within your site.

7   Click OK to attach Accessible_Design.css to your document.

8   Save your work.

Add a Contact Form

Next, you're going to place a contact form into contact.cfm, then set the
form's attributes so that it will be connected to the form processing page.
Don't worry about the processing part just yet; you'll get to that in the
"Build a Form-to-Email Processing Page with Server Behaviors" section.

1   Open, or make active, contact.cfm.

2   Click the Form button in the Forms category of the Insert bar to
    insert a blank <form> to start working with.

3   In the Property inspector for the form tag, click the Folder icon next to the Action field and select thankyou.cfm.

The other attributes available on the form's Property inspector can be left at their default state, as they do not need to be changed for the processing script to work its magic.

4   Save your work.

Add a Table for Form Layout

The form fields that you need depend on the information you want to gather. For this project, imagine that you are working for a video rental store, DWMagic Video Rentals. You need to gather the customer's name, email address, preferred video media, favorite genres, preferred movie ratings, and a catch-all comments field for additional information the customer is willing to share.

You'll be inserting a seven-row by two-column table to make the visual layout of the form easier to manage, and then inserting description text for the visitors' entries in the form fields that you add in the next section.

1   Click the Insert Table button on the Common category of the Insert bar.

2   Type 7 in the Rows field, 2 in the Columns field, delete any entry in the Table Width field, delete any entry in the Border Thickness field, and select Left in the Header section. Click OK.

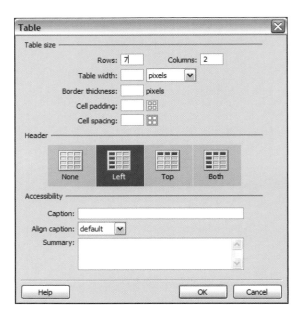

3   In the first column of the table, type the following items, each in its own row, leaving the last row empty:

Name

Email

Preferred Media

Genre

Acceptable Ratings

Comments

Adding Text Fields

The site visitor needs to enter his name and email address so that the video store can contact the visitor when a movie fitting his preferences is in stock. Because this information is fairly short text, you can use text fields to accept the visitor's information.

1   Switch back to the Forms category of the Insert bar.

2   In the second column of the table, in the first row, insert a text field by clicking the Text Field button in the Insert bar.

3   With the field still selected, type <u>fullName</u> into the field on the left of the Property inspector under TextField.

4   Repeat steps 2 and 3 in the second row of the right column, this time using <u>emailAddress</u> as the entry in the field under TextField.

5   Save your work.

Note: Names of form fields should start with a letter, and they should have no spaces or special characters in them.

Inserting a Radio Button Group

Some pieces of information that need to be gathered from site visitors can be only one of a set of mutually exclusive options. Adding a radio button group to your form is the right solution. A visitor can select only one of the items within a radio button group. If the visitor tries to select a different item, then the previous item selected becomes unchecked, leaving only the new selection checked.

1   In the right column for the Preferred Media row, insert a set of radio buttons by clicking the Radio Group button in the Insert bar.

2   In the Radio Group dialog, type <u>preferredMedia</u> in the Name field.

3   Click in the field immediately under Label, then type <u>DVD</u>, tab over into the Value field, and type <u>DVD</u>. Press Tab again, to move into the next row. Type <u>VHS</u> in the Label and Value fields. Under Lay Out Using, select Line Breaks. Click OK.

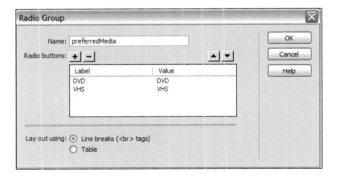

4   Save your work.

Note: The labels and values for a radio button or a select menu do not have to be the same. You can have a label of Mint Chocolate Chip in a form asking about ice cream preferences, but have the value of that item be MCC, or it could even be a number. Just be sure you use values that make sense to the person reading the email, because the value is sent by the form processing script, not the label.

Inserting a Select List and Assigning the Default Display Item

If the information you need to gather dictates that the user select one item out of many options, then a select list field is a great choice.

1   In the cell next to Genre, insert a select list by clicking the List/Menu button on the Insert bar.

2   With the select menu still selected, type <u>genre</u> in the field under List/Menu in the Property inspector to give the menu a name.

3   Click the List Values button in the Property inspector for the select list to open the List Values dialog.

4   In the field under the Item Label column, type <u>Select a genre</u>, then type <u>None</u> under the Value column. In the next row of the field, type <u>Action</u> under Item Label, and <u>Action</u> under Value. Repeat for <u>Comedy</u>, <u>Drama</u>, <u>Mystery</u>, and <u>Western</u>. Click OK.

5   In the Property inspector for the select menu, click the entry for Select a Genre in the Initially Selected field.

Note: As a default, many browsers will show the first item in a select list when the page is loaded. By selecting an item in the initially selected field, you can specify to the browser which item to display when the form is first viewed. Using this option, you can select items in a list that are not at the top entry in the select list.

---

6   Save your work.

Adding Check Boxes for Multiple Selectable Options

If you have a piece of data for which you need only a yes or no answer, then a check box is the preferred form field for gathering that data. In the case of DWMagic Video Rentals, the visitor may want to have zero, one, several, or all of the various movie ratings to be considered when the video store is making suggestions for movies. Because each rating calls for a yes (include) or no (do not include) answer, a check box for each available rating needs to be offered in the contact form.

1   In the cell to the right of Acceptable Ratings, insert a check box by clicking the Checkbox button on the Insert bar.

2   With the check box still selected, name it <u>G</u> and set the Checked value to <u>Yes</u> by typing in the appropriate fields in the Property inspector.

3   Place the insertion point to the right of the check box, and type <u>G</u>. Press Shift+Enter to insert a line break to move to the next line.

4   Repeat steps 1 through 3, this time naming the boxes <u>PG</u>, <u>PG13</u>, and <u>R</u>, and typing <u>Yes</u> for the Checked values.

5   Save your work.

Placing a Textarea to Accept Freeform Text Entry

Sometimes you want to be able to accept multiple words or even paragraphs of text from a visitor, such as for customer comments or suggestions. For this type of information gathering, a textarea is perfect.

1   In the cell to the right of Comments, insert a textarea by clicking the Textarea button on the Insert bar.

2   To give the textarea a name, type <u>comments</u> in the field under Textarea on the Property inspector.

3   Save your work.

Placing Buttons to Submit and Reset the Form

When your visitors have finished filling out your form, they need some way in which to send the information on to you—the submit button. They also may need a method with which to start over again if they gave incorrect information—the reset button.

1   In the right column of the last row, insert a button by clicking the Button button in the Insert bar. Delete Submit from the Button name field.

You're deleting the name in this field because of the way forms work. When the form is submitted, if the submit button has a name, that name is sent along with the other field names and their values to the processing page. Because the script in the processing page will be sending all the names of the fields and their values to an email address, there is no need to also send the name of the submit button, as that isn't relevant information to the recipient.

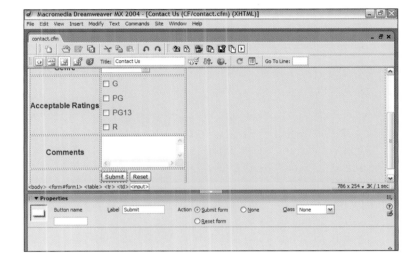

Note: Input buttons inserted through the Insert bar are by default submit buttons. Look in the Property inspector immediately after inserting a button and you'll see the Submit Form option selected. You'll also see that you have the option to change the button to a reset button by selecting Reset Form. When a form is viewed online and there is a reset button, clicking that button will return the form to the same state that it was in when the page first loaded. You also have the option to change the button type to None, which means the button doesn't perform an action whatsoever. This last type is often used to apply custom JavaScript functionality to a form, such as adding fields together or opening browser windows.

2   Next to the submit button, insert another button from the Insert bar, and in the Property inspector for that button, select Reset Form.

3   Save contact.cfm, then upload contact.cfm and thankyou.cfm. Preview contact.cfm to see if there are any noticeable errors. Click the Submit button.

If the browser is taken to thankyou.cfm when you click Submit, then you have correctly hooked up the contact form to the as-yet non-functioning processing page.

Build a Form-to-Email Processing Page with Server Behaviors

Now that your completed form is connected to the soon-to-be form processing page, you need to build the proper functionality into thankyou.cfm so that it can send an email with the values the site visitor entered into the form in contact.cfm. First, you'll insert some text into the form processor page that thanks the visitor for filling out the contact form. Then, you will need to add some code that can process the form entries and send out an email for use by DWMagic Video Rentals staff. You could hand-code everything needed to accomplish the task, but there's no magic in that. An extension can do the grunt work for you—all you need to do is to specify a couple of options, and your form processing page is complete.

1   Open thankyou.cfm.

2   Type <u>Thank you for contacting DWMagic Video Rentals</u>. Press Enter to start a new paragraph, then type <u>As soon as a movie that matches your preferences arrives, we will inform you.</u>.

3   Open the Server Behaviors panel by using Window > Server Behaviors (Ctrl+F9/Cmd+F9).

4   Click the (+) button on the Server Behaviors panel to display a list of available Server Behaviors and select DWMagic > DWMagic CF Mailer.

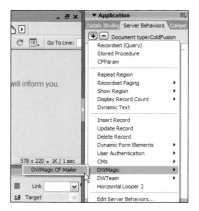

If you are using one of the other server models, then the proper selection here will be DWMagic ASP_VB Mailer or DWMagic PHP Mailer.

5   In the DWMagic CF Mailer dialog, enter an email address to have the form submission sent to (in this example, suggestions@dwmagic.com) in the To Email field, then enter the from address (in this example, webform@dwmagic.com) in the From Email field, and Web form submission in the Subject field.

Use valid email addresses in the To Email and From Email fields that are appropriate for your clients or your company. The To field is the address that you want the form's entries sent to, and the From field is the address that you want the email to appear to be sent from.

6   Save, and then upload contact.cfm and thankyou.cfm to your remote site.

7   Browse to contact.cfm, fill out the form, then click the Submit button.

8   Check the email box for the address that you entered in the To Email field of the DWMagic CF Mailer dialog.

Editing an Existing Server Behavior

Down the road, your client may want the form entries sent to a different email address than the one originally set in the Thank You page. You can make the changes by editing the existing application of the DWMagic Mailer server behavior.

1   Open the Server Behaviors panel.

2   Double-click the DWMagic CF Mailer entry in the Server Behaviors panel. The DWMagic CF Mailer dialog and the fields will be automatically populated with options you set when last you applied/edited the server behavior.

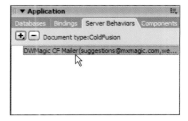

3   Make your changes as needed, click the OK button, save, upload, and you're finished.

Now Try This

By now you've learned how to use Dreamweaver's sample CSS style sheets to give your pages a styling jumpstart; create a ColdFusion, ASP VBScript, or PHP Contact Us page with a form on it; use Dreamweaver form objects to add text fields, radio buttons, a select menu, check boxes, a textarea, and buttons to your contact page form; and build a Thank You page using the DWMagic Mailer Server Behavior that can process site visitors' form submissions on the Contact Us page, and then send an email containing those form entries.

Here are some ideas on how to apply the skills you've learned or use the project you've completed in other ways:

- If you'd like to be able to send the resulting email to more than one email address, for example, enter a comma-separated list of email addresses into the To Email field of the DWMagic Mailer dialog.

- If you have to create a new page with a form on it that needs its contents sent to the email address set in your existing form processing page, then set the Action of the form in the new page to point to the form processing page.

Setting Styles Dynamically

Daniel Short is the chief developer for Web Shorts Site Design and a devoted Team Macromedia Volunteer. He helps to maintain several HTML and Dreamweaver reference sites including Dreamweaver FAQ.com, for which he created the style changer and all ASP functionality, including the Snippets Exchange and the DWfaq Store.

Daniel Short

Several years ago—I can hardly believe it—Angela asked me if I could build a style changer for DWfaq.com to make it possible for every author to have their own color scheme. That little adventure led me to discover the wonders of Cascading Style Sheets and how you can use them to change every facet of a site by swapping out a single file. Further playing led to making it possible to do everything on the server so that it's totally transparent to the user.

My experience with the DWfaq style changer gave me the idea to use one on my own site, and eventually to figure out how to easily explain the process to DWfaq users. With Massimo's help, you now have an extension that will handle it all for you. And even if you never use a style changer on your own sites, the steps taken to plan and organize a style changer-enabled site will serve you well by helping you build your CSS skill set.

It Works Like This

With the wonders of Cascading Style Sheets (CSS), you can completely separate a document's content from its formatting. This not only allows you to quickly update a site's look by updating a single file, it also provides a way to let a user select from a list of desired styles for a site, or even pick and choose their own colors if the site allows them. Here are the basic steps for the project:

1 Build a separate style sheet for each color scheme for the site.

2 Create images for each of the three color schemes using Fireworks.

3 Use the CSS Switcher extensions provided with this project to build a Style Switcher in ASP, VBScript, or ColdFusion.

   For the duration of this project, we'll be using ASP VBScript (.asp). You might want to follow along using ColdFusion with the appropriate file extension (.cfm).

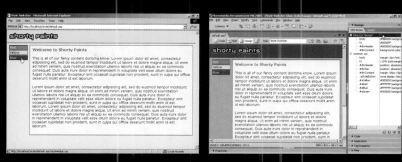

You can build a separate style sheet with each color selected (here we're moving from yellow to blue) using various CSS styles.

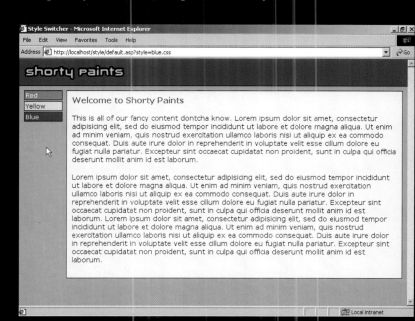

Now we've selected blue and finalized the page.

Preparing to Work

To prepare for this project, you will need to do the following:

1 All of the files used in this project are located in the **Projects/09/** folder on the CD. You should also have Fireworks installed for some simple image manipulation for each of the color schemes you're going to build.

2 Install the CSS Style Switcher Extension, **CSS Switcher.mxp**, in the **Projects/09/Extensions/** folder. See Appendix A, "Installing Extensions," for more information.

2 Copy the necessary files for this project from the **Projects/09/** folder to your hard drive. The finished folder contains a fully working copy of the project, but all you need to get started is the **assets** folder and **default.asp**.

3 Define a new site using the Projects/09/ copy as your site root. In the site setup, be sure to define your testing server in order to take advantage of the server-side language you choose to use. You can use ASP VBScript or ColdFusion.

Browser Compatibility

The style switcher will work as well as your styles are written. You just have to be sure that you properly plan out your separate style sheets for each color scheme. The only thing necessary for it to work is that visitors must have cookies enabled. Checking to see whether cookies are enabled on a client's machine is outside the scope of this chapter, so I'll leave that to you.

Setting Up Your Base Styles

In order to get started, you need a base style sheet to start from, which then becomes the basis for every other style sheet you're going to use. In this section, you're going to take the style sheet I've already built for you and make it usable for the rest of your color schemes.

1 The first thing that is needed is the base site with the default color scheme, but I've already taken care of that part for you. Open **default.asp** in Dreamweaver. This is the base color scheme for Shorty Paints, a wonderful shade of yellow.

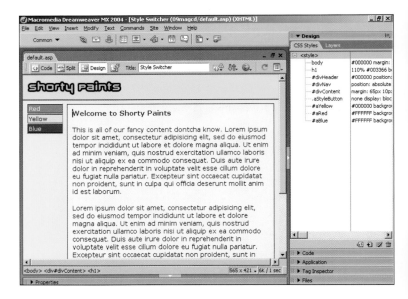

2 Open the CSS Styles panel. In the CSS Styles panel, all of the styles are listed under a `<style>` tag heading. This is because all of the styles are currently embedded directly into the page.

3 Right-click/Ctrl-click the top `<style>` block in the CSS Styles panel, and choose Export. Browse to the folder containing your page, and save the style sheet as <u>common.css</u>. This gets all the styles outside of the base document.

4 Repeat step 3, but name the CSS file <u>yellow.css</u>.

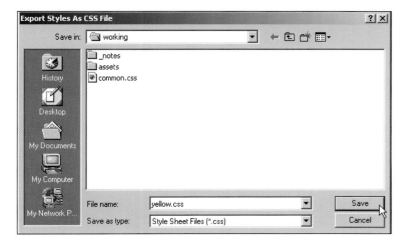

5 Now that you have two duplicate style sheets, you need to remove the embedded styles and link the two new style sheets. In the CSS Styles panel, right-click the `<style>` block again, but this time choose Delete.

6 Click the Attach Style Sheet button, the far left button at the bottom of the CSS Styles panel, and attach the common.css file using the Link method.

Tip: If you have multiple subfolders throughout your site, it's often best to use Site Root relative links with the CSS Switcher to ensure your CSS links are always correct.

7 Click the Options menu in the CSS Styles panel and choose Design-time. Attach yellow.css by clicking the (+) icon in the Design Time Style Sheets dialog and browsing to the yellow.css file.

You should see `design` next to the yellow.css label in the CSS Styles panel. Your page should look exactly like it did before you exported the style sheets.

You need to use a Design Time Sheet at this point because you don't want the yellow.css actually embedded into the page—you'll be switching it out with additional style sheets later on.

Note: Design Time Style Sheets are one of the best things Macromedia engineers ever dreamed up. They allow you to view a page using style sheets that aren't actually linked to your page in the code. They're used for working visually in Dreamweaver only, and your site's visitors will never see them.

8   Open common.css and remove any properties that contain color information.

You are starting to break apart the style sheets. The common.css file will contain all of the positioning information and yellow.css will contain just the color information. Separating the positioning and color information will make it easier to develop new color schemes later on.

Tip: To quickly open a style sheet, simply double-click the style sheet name in the CSS Styles panel.

Note: The ability to break things apart into separate style sheets is another huge advantage of using CSS. Splitting out all of the color information makes it easy to manipulate only those properties you need to.

You'll have to remove color properties, background color properties, and even borders from common.css if you plan on changing these per style. The only exception will be the ids for the three links that will handle the style changer and their border style, #aRed, #aYellow, #aBlue, and .aStyleButton. These styles will remain the same across all three site color schemes.

9   Open yellow.css, and remove any rules and properties that *don't* contain color information. Be sure to also remove the four definitions for the style changer buttons.

In the previous step you were removing just the properties you didn't need. This time you'll need to remove complete rules, such as #divNav, that don't contain any color definition at all.

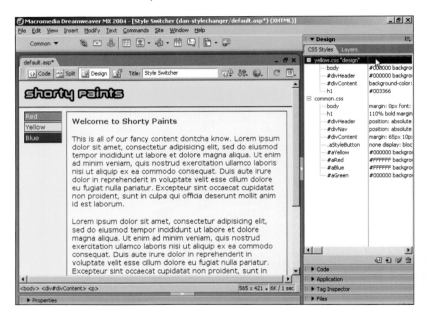

10   Save both common.css and yellow.css.

Build Color Scheme Style Sheets

Now that everything is broken out correctly, you're probably starting to see how you're going to set up your new colors. You have one style sheet for positioning, and you need one style sheet for each color scheme. In this section you're going to build the additional style sheets for each of the color schemes.

1   Right-click/Ctrl-click yellow.css in the Files panel, and choose Edit > Duplicate to create a copy of yellow.css. Repeat this step once more to create another duplicate of yellow.css. You now have new style sheets ready to go: Copy of yellow.css and Copy [2] of yellow.css.

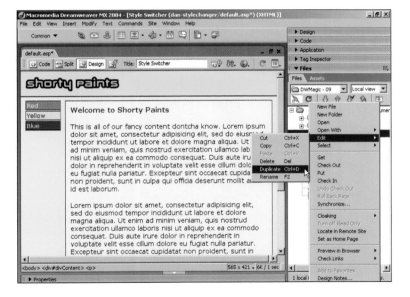

2   Rename the duplicates to <u>red.css</u> and <u>blue.css</u>. You can either right-click/Ctrl-click the file and choose Edit > Rename, or click the file once, pause, and then click the file again.

3   In the CSS Styles panel, choose Options > Design-time. (The icon in the right corner of the expanded panel with the three little lines and a down arrow is called the Options menu.) Highlight yellow.css, and click the (–) button to remove the style sheet. Click the (+) button and add red.css. Your page should look exactly the same as it did when yellow.css was attached, but have red.css attached instead.

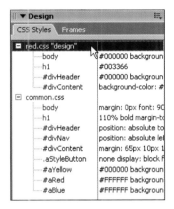

4   Either double-click the red.css "design" listing in the CSS Styles panel and edit the style sheet manually, or right-click/Ctrl-click each entry in red.css and choose Edit to use the CSS Styles Definition dialog. Open each style rule in red.css, and pick whatever shades of red you want for colors and background colors by using the Color Picker. Save the red.css file.

Tip: You can also use the Tag inspector panel (Window > Tag Inspector or F9) to make changes to CSS rules. Just select a rule from the CSS Styles panel and the Tag inspector will change to allow you to edit your CSS rules.

Whichever route you decide to take, your red.css file should end up looking much like the following code, with all of the yellow colors changed to shades of red:

Listing 9.1

```
body {
      background-color: #FFA8A8;
      color: #000000;
}
#divHeader {
      background-color: #FF0000;
      color: #000000;
      border-bottom: 1px solid #000000;
}
#divContent {
      background-color: #FFF4F4;
      border: 1px solid #000000;
}
h1 {
      color: #FF0000;
}
```

5   Choose Options > Design-time, remove red.css, and add blue.css. Change all of your colors to shades of blue either directly in the CSS file or through the CSS Editor. This sets up the blue style sheet.

Listing 9.2

```
body {
      background-color: #A8A8FF;
      color: #000000;
}
#divHeader {
      background-color: #0000FF;
      color: #000000;
      border-bottom: 1px solid #000000;
}
#divContent {
      background-color: #F4F4FF;
      border: 1px solid #000000;
}
h1 {
      color: #0000FF;
}
```

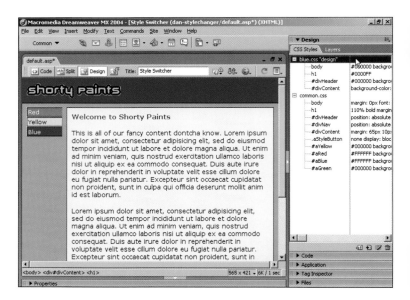

6   Save your work.

Creating Color-Friendly Images

The first thing you probably noticed at the end of the previous section is the rather atrocious anti-aliasing around the Shorty Paints logo. When this image was exported from Fireworks, it had a transparent background set to match the yellow of the default site color scheme. When you switch style sheets, the image still has some remnants of that yellow color, used as a matte by Fireworks to make things blend nicely. This creates a major problem, which you'll address by exporting duplicates of the logo and changing some of your CSS rules. Instead of embedding the image on the page, you're going to make it a background image on divHeader.

Note: One problem with switching images as backgrounds appears when trying to print the page. Background images may or may not show. To find out how to get around this limitation, check out the "Now Try This" section at the end of this project.

1   Open **layout.png** (in the **assets** folder of your site) in Fireworks. The first thing you'll notice is that there are three layers, one for each color scheme: Red, Yellow, and Blue. The Yellow layer should be visible.

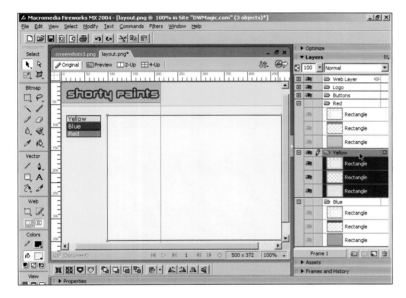

2   Hide the Yellow layer by clicking the eye icon next to the Yellow layer name, and show the red layer by clicking the eye icon next to the Red layer name.

3   Right-click/Ctrl-click on the slice on top of the Shorty Paints logo and choose Export Selected Slice.

4   In the Export dialog, browse to the assets folder for your site and save the logo as <u>logo-red.gif</u>. Do the same for the blue logo. Hide the Red layer by clicking the eye icon next to the Red layer, and show the Blue layer by clicking the eye icon next to the Blue layer name. Save the image as <u>logo-blue.gif</u> in your site's assets folder. You can now save the document and close Fireworks.

5   Back in Dreamweaver, click the Shorty Paints logo to select it and press the Delete key.

6   Open the CSS Styles panel if it's not already open. Make sure the blue.css style sheet is still attached as a Design Time Style Sheet. Right-click/Ctrl-click the #divHeader entry, and choose Edit.

7   Go to the Background category of the CSS Style Definition dialog and browse to logo-blue.gif for the Background Image. Choose no-repeat for the Repeat entry. Click OK to apply the changes.

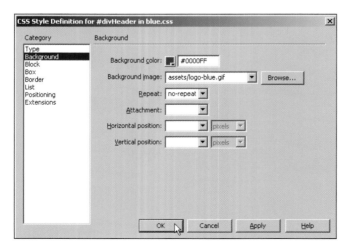

8   Save the CSS file and your page should now look exactly like it did before you removed the logo, only without the ugly yellow matting.

9   Perform the same operation for red.css and yellow.css. You can either change the Design Time Style Sheet to the appropriate sheet and set the logo for #divHeader in each style sheet, or edit the style sheets directly. When you're finished, you should have yellow.css attached as a Design Time Style Sheet.

Note: Please explore all of the properties located in the background category of the CSS Style Definition dialog. Choosing no-repeat prevents the background image from repeating at all. It's also possible to attach a background to a particular side of an element and even move the background right and down a certain number of pixels. The sky's the limit.

Using the CSS Switcher Extensions

It's finally time to get to the good stuff...applying the Server Behaviors. This section will show you how to apply a Style Switcher to a page, and how to build links to switch to a specific style.

1   With default.asp still open, open the Server Behaviors panel.

2   Click the (+) icon in the Server Behaviors panel and choose DWfaq > CSS Switcher.

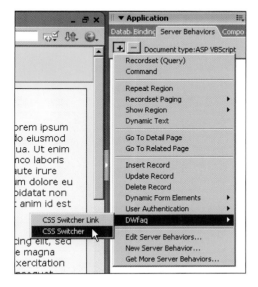

3   Click the Browse button, and choose the yellow.css file. Click OK. This will load yellow.css if a user hasn't chosen any specific style. When you click OK, the CSS Switcher server behavior should display in the Server Behaviors panel.

4   Choose the <a> tag for the Red button, click the (+) icon in the Server Behaviors panel, and choose DWfaq > CSS Switcher Link. The CSS Switcher Link server behavior adds a link back to the current page with a querystring added to the end that tells the CSS Switcher which style sheet to load.

5   Click the Browse button, browse to the red.css file, and click OK. If you have files in multiple folders that will be using the CSS Switcher, be sure to link to your CSS files via a Site Root relative link, and not a Document relative link. If you use a document-relative link, then pages located in subfolders of your site won't display correctly because the path generated by the CSS Switcher Link server behavior won't be correct.

6   Perform the same actions for the Yellow and Blue buttons: Click the <a> tag in the tag selector, and apply the CSS Switcher Link server behavior to each button. Your Server Behaviors panel should now list the CSS Switcher and three instances of CSS Switcher Link. Browse to the page on your server and click away.

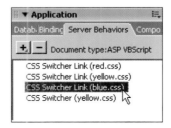

7   Save your work.

Now Try This

By now you've learned how to build color scheme style sheets, create color-friendly images, and use the CSS Switcher extensions.

Here are some ideas on how to apply the skills you've learned or use the project you've completed in other ways:

- One problem with a standard CSS Switcher is that you're only changing CSS files. If you have a lot of images that you need to switch as well, you can't depend on a CSS file full of background images. You'll need to change the actual physical image paths (take a look at the huge number of styles at www.dwfaq.com and choose My DWfaq's Style from the My DWfaq menu). A little hand coding to add a variable for a folder name containing all of the images for the Yellow, Red, and Blue color schemes will enable you to embed images for each of the appropriate color schemes. For an example, check out the files in the **Projects/09/NowTryThis/** folder. Just a warning, some of the modifications will break the server behaviors in the Server Behaviors panel.

- Feeling adventurous? Why not have the style sheets be completely user customizable, down to colors and font sizes? It's entirely possible to have a user complete a form and write custom style sheets based off his or her input.

Creating a Rotating Ad System in ASP.NET

Joel Martinez

Joel Martinez creates enterprise-level web applications using the .NET Framework (among other technologies). He is the founder of the Orlando .NET User Group and is also a partner at Community MX.

Since my early days in the programming scene, I've been working on the web. One of the recurring issues that I've had to deal with in one way or the other is online advertisements. And I know that this is a topic that many readers can relate to.

When I was given this assignment, I wanted to show everyone how amazing ASP.NET is. I am amazed more and more every day at the depth of functionality that is available to me as an ASP.NET developer. Unfortunately, due to space constraints in these pages, I had to cut out a few of the things I wanted to highlight in this project. Even so, I think you'll be able to see the power and functionality that's already built into the framework, and the ease with which you can make custom components. Hopefully, it will spark a curiosity that will further expose you to the .NET framework.

It Works Like This

The true test of a tool is how much time it actually saves you. ASP.NET has many features that abstract some of the repetitive functions that must go into all web applications. By using these rapid application development features, you will be free to focus on functionality rather than repeating code from project to project. Here are the basic steps of the project:

1 Build an ad-rotating module for your web site in ASP.NET. You will use the built-in ad rotator control that comes with ASP.NET for the display of the ads.

2 Create an upload page for ad administration using the **MX Magic Upload Extension** that comes on the CD.

3 Prepare a database connection to track click-through traffic.

4 Write ADO.NET code to track click-throughs.

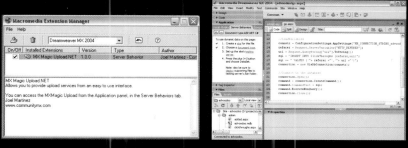

In order to create an upload page for this project, you need to import some extensions and insert some ASP.NET code.

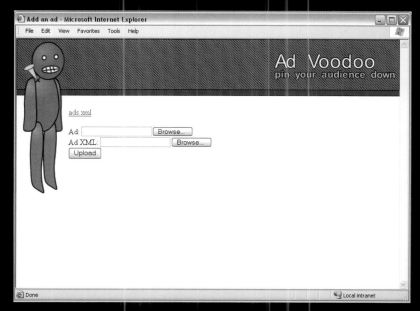

Here's the final page with ASP.NET code implemented.

Preparing to Work

To prepare for this project, you will need to do the following:

1 Install IIS if you are going to test your files locallly.

2 Install the .NET framework SDK setup, which can be found online at www.dwmagic.com/go/8. The setup is very straightforward. Accept all of the default options by clicking Next through each step of the installation.

3 Install the extension **MXMagic Upload.mxp**, located in the **Projects/10/Extensions** folder on the accompanying CD. See Appendix A, "Installing Extensions," for more information.

4 Import the example files included on the accompanying CD in the **Projects/10** directory. This includes the XML file that you will be creating, the example files, a click-through Access database, and some sample image banners you can use. With the software installed, you can set up the site in IIS and Dreamweaver.

5 Create a Virtual Directory in IIS called advoodoo.

6 Open the IIS Admin Snap-In by choosing Start > Control Panel, click Performance and Maintenance, click Administrative Tools, and then double-click Internet Information Services.

7 Right-click the <computername>/Web Sites/Default Web Site node, and choose New > Virtual Directory.

8 In the Virtual Directory Creation Wizard, enter advoodoo for the Alias and click Next. This will allow you to access the project using http://localhost/advoodoo.

9 Point the alias to the directory on your local machine where you copied the project files. Click the Browse button, browse to the correct folder, and click Next. Click Next on the next screen to accept the defaults and then click Finish.

10 Create a site in Dreamweaver using the ASP.NET C# or VB server model.

A Word on Workstations

At the time of this writing, the preferred OS for ASP.NET development is Windows 2000/XP Professional. The reason is that IIS comes on the OS installation disc. XP Home, although similar to XP Pro, does not have the IIS component. If you need to use XPHome, you might install a lightweight (and open-source) ASP.NET web server called Cassini that works on any Windows 2000 or XP-based system. You can find it at www.dwmagic.com/go/9.

Browser Compatibility

The HTML generated by the ad rotator control is completely cross-browser and XHTML-compliant.

Serving Rotating Banner Ads

ASP.NET's server controls are revolutionary in the sense that you have a lot of functionality built into what have historically been considered client-side tools. Now, buttons and text boxes can execute server-side code through events. This makes development quite a bit easier as you no longer have to deal with repetitive issues, such as controlling the flow of code depending on whether you want different code to run based on a user's action. Many have compared the new thought process with JavaScript or Windows forms because you must now think in terms of events.

One of these much-touted controls is the *ad rotator control*. By using a simple XML data source, deployment of this control couldn't be easier. You begin by creating a new XML document to serve as the ad data store. The definitions in this file dictate which banner ads get shown.

1   Create a new XML document.

2   Choose the Basic Page category in the New Document dialog, pick XML in the list on the right side, and click the Create button. The structure of the XML document you will make next is very simple.

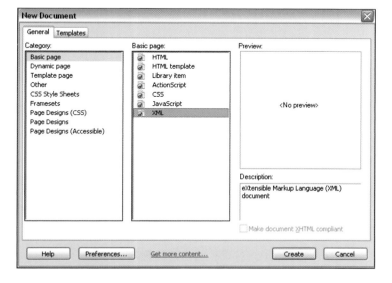

Note: Each element in the **ads.xml** file is case-sensitive. Be sure to copy each tag exactly as you see it or else the ad rotator will not see the data.

3   Add the outer Advertisements element:

Listing 10.1

```
<?xml version="1.0" encoding="iso-8859-7"? >
<Advertisements>
</Advertisements>
```

4   Within the Advertisements element, create an Ad element:

Listing 10.2

```
<Ad>
</Ad>
```

5   Add the five elements contained in every Ads tag.

ImageURL is the location of your image. Flash ads are not supported, so this must point to a regular image. The URL can be either document-relative or a full path. Remember that if you are using a document-relative path to the image, it must be relative to the page that the ad will appear in.

Listing 10.3

```
<ImageUrl>
</ImageUrl>
```

NavigateUrl is where the viewer will be redirected when the banner ad is clicked.

Listing 10.4

```
<NavigateUrl>
</NavigateUrl>
```

AlternateText will populate the image's alt attribute.

Listing 10.5

```
<AlternateText>
</AlternateText>
```

Impressions dictates how often the ad shows in relation to other ads in the XML file. Though it's not necessary, it is best to make all the impressions add up to 100, as if you were using percentages. This just makes it easier to manage your impressions.

Listing 10.6

```
<Impressions>
</Impressions>
```

Keyword allows you to run different ad campaigns by having similar ads that have the same keyword. One common use is to differentiate horizontal ads from vertical ads. This way, you can have them all in the same ad file, but keep them conveniently separated.

Listing 10.7

```
<Keyword>
</Keyword>
```

Here is an example ad file:

Listing 10.8

```
<Advertisements>
    <Ad>
        <ImageUrl>ads/rastaroni.jpg</ImageUrl>

        <NavigateUrl>http://www.rastaroni.com</NavigateUrl>
        <AlternateText>The Rasta Man's Treat</AlternateText>
        <Impressions>55</Impressions>
        <Keyword>advoodoo</Keyword>
    </Ad>
    <Ad>
        <ImageUrl>ads/invaluable.gif</ImageUrl>

        <NavigateUrl>http://www.vooodooo.com</NavigateUrl>
        <AlternateText>There are some things the law
    ➥won't allow, For everything else there's
    ➥Voodoo</AlternateText>
        <Impressions>45</Impressions>
        <Keyword>advoodoo</Keyword>
    </Ad>
</Advertisements>
```

6   Save the file as ads.xml in your site root directory. Now that you have the data source ready, you can start serving ads with one simple line of code.

7   Create a new ASP.NET C# or VB file in Dreamweaver by selecting File > New and choosing ASP.NET C# or ASP.NET VB from the Dynamic Page category.

8   Switch to Code view and inside the `<body>` tags add the following line of code:

```
<asp:adrotator AdvertisementFile="ads.xml" runat="server" />
```

This server control will rotate the ads that are present in the ads.xml file.

9   Save the file as showad.aspx and preview the page in a browser.

It's as simple as that. As you refresh the page, you can see that the ad will rotate at random. The values you define in the `<Impressions>` tag will dictate how often the ad shows up in relation to other documents.

Uploading Files by Applying a Server Behavior

There's one thing that highly paid ASP.NET consultants will not want you to know: Anything is possible with the .NET framework. The sky is really the limit. File uploading in a web application was one of those things that was usually relegated to third-party components or complicated scripts in the olden days of classic ASP. I will concede that ColdFusion got it right with its built-in file uploading capabilities way before .NET came out, but aside from that, it was one of those things that you'd either have to pay for or be a guru to implement.

No more. The Dreamweaver extension you installed in "Preparing to Work" (**MXMagic Upload.mxp**) makes it as easy as applying a server behavior to your page to provide upload services to your application. Although it is very simple to do it without the aid of a third-party tool, this extension removes the need for you to write any code whatsoever.

1   Create a new ASP.NET C# or ASP.NET VB page. The server behavior inserts a custom tag into your page, so it doesn't matter what language you're using.

2   In Code view, place a server-side web form on the page.

Listing 10.9

```
<form runat="server">
</form>
```

3   With the cursor within the form tag, apply the server behavior (MXMagic Upload) by clicking the (+) icon in the Server Behaviors panel (Windows > Server Behaviors or Ctrl+F9) and choosing MX Magic Upload.

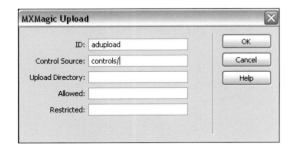

4   Supply the server behavior with a unique id and the location where you would like to store the custom control (Control Source). If you leave Control Source blank, the control will be placed in a "Controls" directory by default.

If you'd like to have more than one upload control on the page, you must supply a different id. Refer to the server behavior's Help message for information on the rest of the fields in the interface.

Note: When applied, the MXMagic Upload server behavior has no visual representation within Dreamweaver's Design view.

The server behavior will copy a file (**mxmagicupload.ascx**) to the directory you specify in the Control Source text box. You must make sure you upload this file to your testing/production server.

The allowed and restricted fields accept a comma-separate string of allowed and disallowed extensions the user can upload.

When the server behavior is applied, it will place a file upload input control on your web form. The value that you supply in the server behavior Upload Directory field will dictate where the user's file will be uploaded.

5   Add an asp:Button server control to the page. With your cursor after the <MXMagic:upload/>, Ctrl-click the asp:Button icon in the ASP.NET category of the Insert bar. Set the text for the button to Upload.

Listing 10.10

```
<asp:Button text="Upload" runat="server" />
```

In all actuality, it could be any server control that will initiate a post back.

Note: By default, the maximum file size that you may upload is around 4MB. If for some reason you would like to change this limit, you must do it in your web.config file. The web.config file is usually placed in the root of your site, but you can place them in subdirectories as well. Add the following <system.web> entry after your <configuration> tag:

Listing 10.11

```
<configuration>
    <system.web>
    <httpRuntime maxRequestLength="10000" />
    </system.web>
</configuration>
```

This snippet raises the limit to 10,000KB (approximately 10MB).

Creating an Upload Page for Ad Administration

Now that you've gone over how to use the MXMagic Upload.NET extension, you will put it to practical use. A simple admin page will allow you to upload new images and a new ad file.

Note: A few sample ads are provided in the **Projects/10/images** folder on the accompanying CD.

Because the MXMagic Upload extension does not have a graphical representation in Dreamweaver, you should be in Code view when applying the extension so you see what is being inserted.

1   Begin by creating a subdirectory in your site called <u>admin</u>.

2   Create a new ASP.NET file (either C# or VB.NET), and save it in the admin directory with the name <u>addad.aspx</u>.

3   Within the <body> tags of addad.aspx, insert a web form. Every server control you add from here on out should be placed within this <form runat="server"> tag.

Listing 10.12

```
<form runat="server">
</form>
```

4   Type the words <u>New Ad</u> directly after the opening <form> tag and then apply the MXMagic Upload server behavior. Use <u>../controls</u> as the Control Source, because you are working from within the /admin subdirectory.

Because this is the upload control that will upload new ads, you should restrict what kinds of files will be uploaded. Simply give a comma-separated list of allowed extensions. In this case, use <u>jpg,gif</u>.

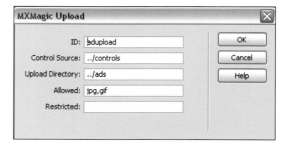

5 Below the new ad control, type the words <u>Ad XML file:</u> and apply the MXMagic Upload server behavior.

Give the new control a different ID than the first upload control. Use the same Control Source value as you did for Step 4. You want to upload the ads.xml file above the admin directory, so use the value <u>../</u> in the Upload Directory field. The only extension that should be allowed is .xml, because you should be uploading only the ads.xml file in this control.

When you apply the server behavior, it will notify you that it wants to overwrite the mxmagicupload.ascx file that was placed there the first time. Because you have not changed the file, you can choose to overwrite the file.

6 Add an asp:Button to trigger the file uploads:

Listing 10.13

```
<asp:Button Text="Upload" runat="server" />
```

No event handler is needed because the mxmagic:upload control will handle itself on postback.

7 Create a new link to the ads.xml file on the server:

Listing 10.14

```
<a href="../ads.xml">ads.xml</a>
```

With this done, updating your ad service is as easy as visiting your page and uploading a new banner ad, and a new ads.xml that contains the new ad.

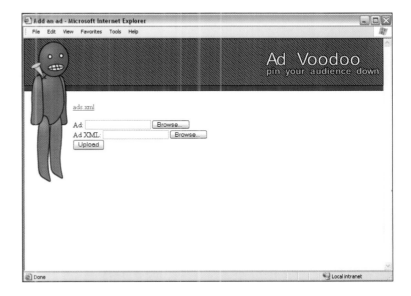

Prepare a Database Connection to Track Click-Through Traffic

Ok, so you've got this nifty rotating ad system. That's great, but now you want to know how many times any given banner is clicked on. This can be easily implemented by creating a redirect page that all banners can point to. This page would simply log the click-through and forward the user to the advertised URL.

You will create a redirect page that you can route all banner clicks through. The data gathered with this page is valuable information for knowing and understanding your readership. By studying it, you can begin to understand what your visitors are interested in and, in turn, tailor your content accordingly.

Because this page will not have an interface, you will not use Dreamweaver's built-in data server behaviors. Instead, you will wire up your own database access code using ADO.NET. Fear not, it's not as scary as it sounds.

1   Copy and paste **advoodoo.mdb** from **Projects/10** on the accompanying CD into your local site. The database is not very complex; in fact, there is only one table in it to hold click-through information.

CAUTION

When dealing with Access databases, it is not a good idea to put them in a publicly accessible folder as is done here. This is just for illustration purposes. All file-based databases should be put in a folder other than your web root.

---

2   Create a new database connection. Refer to Appendix B, "Creating Database Connections," for more information on creating one.

Note: You may access your connection string at any time by using the following code:

```
ConfigurationSettings.AppSettings["MM_CONNECTION_STRING_
➥advoodoo"];
```

Replace advoodoo with whatever you've named your connection.

Writing the ADO.NET Code to Track Click-Throughs

With the database connection set up, you can proceed to the task at hand: writing the code that will track click-through traffic. The script will simply take a QueryString parameter indicating which URL to redirect the user to.

1   Create a new ASP.NET C# file, and save it in the root directory with the name of go.aspx.

2   Erase the default code that Dreamweaver inserts into the page and insert the top-level @ parameters:

Listing 10.15

```
<%@ Page Language="C#" %>
<%@ Import Namespace="System.Data" %>
<%@ Import Namespace="System.Data.OleDb" %>
```

These declare the language being used and import the data namespaces.

3   Begin the server script block and declare the Page_Load event using this code:

Listing 10.16

```
<script runat="server">
protected void Page_Load(Object Src, EventArgs E)
{
```

Truthfully, you could use any one of the page's events (Page_Init, Page_Load, Page_PreRender). There's no real performance boost based on which one you pick, so it doesn't matter.

4   Declare and load your variables with these lines:

Listing 10.17

```
//Declare Variables
string connstr,referer,url,sql;
OleDbConnection connection;
OleDbCommand command;

//LoadVariables
connstr = ConfigurationSettings.AppSettings
➥["MM_CONNECTION_STRING_advoodoo"];
referer = Request.ServerVariables["HTTP_REFERER"];
url = Request.QueryString["url"].ToString();
sql = "INSERT INTO ClickThroughs (referer,url)";
sql += " VALUES ('"+ referer +"','"+ url +"')";
connection = new OleDbConnection(connstr);
```

There are four variables being instantiated here: `connstr`, `referer`, `url`, and `sql`. Notice that you are inserting the `referer` and `url` into the database in the `sql` string. Basically, you're logging where the visitor comes from and where they are going.

5 Add this code to connect to the database and execute your SQL insert statement:

Listing 10.18

```
//Connect to the database
connection.Open();
command = connection.CreateCommand();
command.CommandText = sql;
command.ExecuteNonQuery();
connection.Close();
```

6 Redirect the user and close out the server script block with this code:

Listing 10.19

```
        //Redirect the user
        Response.Redirect(url);
}
</script>
```

7 Point your banner ads (the `<NavigateUrl>` tag in the ads.xml file) to something like `go.aspx?url=http://www.communitymx.com`. This data can be used in a number of ways, not the least of which to show potential advertisers what kind of traffic they can expect to get by advertising on your site.

Now Try This

By now you've learned how to build an ad-rotating module for your web site in ASP.NET, create an administration page for editing your banner ads, and add the ability for your site to track click-throughs for your banner ads.

Here are some ideas on how to apply the skills you've learned or use the project you've completed in other ways:

- Protect the admin directory by using forms authentication. The system we've created here is implicitly insecure. By using forms authentication, you are ensuring that your back-end administration remains safe.

- Create reports to display click-through stats. We've already shown you how to interact with a database using ADO.NET. Take it a step further and add valuable analysis tools to your application.

Creating Dynamic Navigation with Server.Execute

Daniel Short is the chief developer for Web Shorts Site Design and a devoted Team Macromedia Volunteer. He helps to maintain several HTML and Dreamweaver reference sites including Dreamweaver FAQ.com, for which he created the style changer and all ASP functionality, including the Snippets Exchange and the DWfaq Store.

Daniel Short
with artwork from Bryan Teglia

I'm a big fan of modularization. I spend a lot of time on every project doing my best to make everything reusable. After all, why code something twice? And why keep duplicate copies of code on different pages? To that end, I've used server side includes for ages, but I found them lacking when I started to develop more complicated modules for my sites.

When I first started developing my blog, I wanted a fancy calendar showing all the posts for my site. I was continually frustrated by variable clashes and problems with Dreamweaver playing with my recordsets when I was developing it as a standard include. I finally switched to using Server.Execute to load my calendar and was able to work on it completely independent from the rest of my blog. I became a Server.Execute convert.

It Works Like This

In this project, you will create a site with different subsection navigation for each main section. To do this, you will use the `Server.Execute` method found in ASP 3.0 to dynamically incorporate a menu based on which folder of your site a page is contained in. This would be both inefficient and hard to manage if you used standard SSIs. As the user moves from section to section inside the site, the gallery menu will change according to the folder the page is contained in. Here are the basic steps for the project:

1 Design with `<div>` tags to make your site easy to manage.

2 Create the includes to build global navigation elements.

3 Power the Content Switcher with `Server.Execute`.

In this project, you'll design using <div> tags and create includes.

Here is the completed web page with all the items in place.

Preparing to Work

To prepare for this project, you will need to do the following:

1   First, install the Server.Execute Translator extension, **ServerExecute.mxp**, located in the **Projects/11/Extensions** folder on the CD. See Appendix A, "Installing Extensions," for more information.

2   Copy the necessary files from the **Projects** folder on the CD. If you want to start from scratch and work each page as you go through the chapter, copy just the **assets** subfolder from the **Projects/11** folder to a location on your hard drive. If you want to get a sneak peek at the files, copy the entire folder.

3   Define a new site using the Projects/11 copy as your site root. Ensure that you specify ASP VBScript as the server model in your site definition.

4   To build the site structure, create a folder for each main section of the gallery, a folder for includes, a folder for menus, and an assets folder for images and style sheets. The includes folder will have site navigation includes as well as the content switcher, which will use `Server.Execute` to load the menus. The menus folder will hold each section's individual menu.

5   Create a folder for each main section of the gallery: Portraits, Panels, and Whites. Under Panels, add two subfolders: ForSale and Installations. You will use these subfolders for testing the menu as you move deeper into a section of the site.

6   Add a default.asp file to each folder, as well as one file for each submenu you're going to create (name them by section: portraits.asp, panels.asp, and whites.asp). Create a contentswitcher.asp and nav.asp file in the includes directory. These last two will hold the site navigation and the actual content switcher for the site.

Server.Execute() Versus SSI

So what's the real difference between using the `Server.Execute` method and SSIs? Compare the two:

Standard SSIs

Syntax: `<!--#include file/virtual="fileName.asp" -->`

Either a file or virtual attribute is used depending on the type of path. A *file path* is the equivalent of a document relative path in HTML, while a *virtual path* is the same as a root relative path in HTML. The file/virtual path must be static; you cannot use dynamic paths in SSI calls.

When an ASP page is requested from the server, all files called with SSI syntax are parsed before the calling page begins processing, so that the server is certain it has all the code it needs first. This means that if you wrote a conditional statement that implements an include file based on a folder's location, each file would have to be integrated into the page in the server's memory as if it were hard coded before it was executed. If you had ten possible menus, all ten menus would be loaded into memory, but only the one menu (that meets the condition) would be displayed in the browser. That's a lot of wasted memory!

Server.Execute() Method

Syntax: `Server.Execute("fileName.asp")`

Unlike includes that require static paths, you can also use variables inside the `Server.Execute` method, manipulating the path to the page you want to execute as required. This means that something like `Server.Execute(myVariable)` is completely acceptable; something that's impossible with standard includes.

continues

continued

With Server.Execute, the code is executed only when you explicitly tell the server to process it; unlike SSI, Server.Execute is not read into memory before the page is processed. This allows you to execute only the code you need to do the job.

Think of Server.Execute files as mini applications that are entirely self-contained, independent of anything that is happening on the calling page. They must even have their own language declaration. A major difference between the Server.Execute method and SSIs is that files called with the Server.Execute method don't have access to any of the variables on the calling page and they can't pass values back to the calling page. They have access to the Request collections (Form, Querystring, Cookie, and so on) and all Session and Application variables, but that's it. This means that you can handle recordsets and other dynamic data without ever worrying about what's happening on the parent page; there is no risk of variable clashing or other conflicts. Server.Execute allows you to completely debug your files independently without ever adding them to your calling page until you need them and you're certain they work.

Browser Compatibility

The Server.Execute method discussed here is completely browser independent. As long as the server is running ASP 3.0, the code will be processed and displayed according to the browser's capabilities.

Designing with *<div>* Tags and Includes

From a layout perspective, this site is going to be very simple: a <div> for the header, one for navigation, and another for the content. I've provided a CSS file for you to attach that will put all the elements in place. After you've built the complete page, you'll then chop it up to build the main navigational include.

1 Open (or create) a default.asp file at the root of your gallery. This should be a blank ASP/VBScript page.

2 Choose Window > CSS Styles (Shift+F11) to open the CSS Styles panel, click the Attach Style Sheet button at the bottom of the panel, and browse to **assets/styles.css**. Choose the link method and click OK to attach the style sheet.

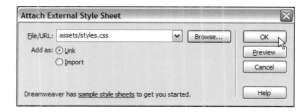

3 Choose Insert > Layout Objects > DIV Tag, or click the Insert DIV Tag object in the Layout category of the Insert bar. For the first <div>, choose divHeader from the ID dropdown; leave everything else at the default and click OK.

A new <div> tag is now added to the page, with the appropriate id attribute. Because the style for this <div> is already defined in the style sheet, it will be properly placed.

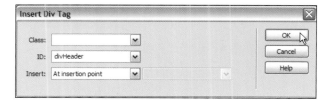

4   Delete the placeholder content (`Content for id "divHeader" Goes Here`) from the `<div>` and insert the **gallery_logo.gif** file from the **assets** folder. You should make the link to the image Site Root relative, because you'll be turning this part of the navigation into an include later on.

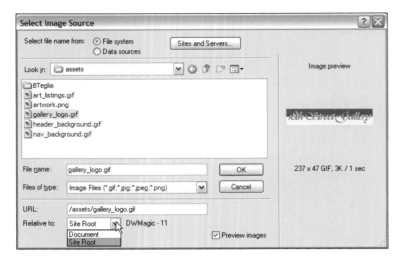

5   Insert the next `<div>` (`divNav`) after `divHeader` using the same Insert Div Tag object. In the Insert Div Tag dialog, choose After Tag and `<div id="divNavContent">` for the Insert options and click OK.

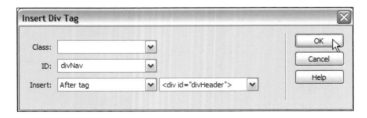

6   Remove the placeholder content from `divNav` and then add the **art_listings.gif** file to the `<div>`. Make sure that the image is added with a Site Root relative path.

7   Insert `divNavContent` directly below art_listings.gif. Click the image and press the right arrow key to move your cursor directly after art_listings.gif and insert `divNavContent` using the Insert Div Tag dialog. Leave the Insert options at their defaults and click OK. There shouldn't be any breaks or paragraphs between the GIF file and `divNavContent`.

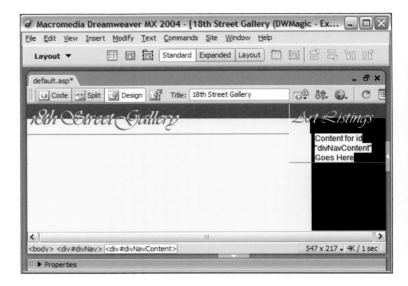

This `<div>` will contain the site's navigation, as well as the content switcher.

8   Remove the placeholder text from `divNavContent`, and type <u>Panels</u>, <u>Portraits</u>, and <u>Whites</u>, pressing Shift+Enter after each to add line breaks. Add links to the default.asp pages under the Panels, Portraits, and Whites folders for each of the respective links. Make sure the links are Site Root relative, not Document relative, by choosing Site Root in the Relative To list in the Select File dialog.

Note: Notice that all of the links are Site Root relative. This allows you to put your navigation in a single include and add that to any file in any folder, and the links will always point to the correct files.

9 Insert the final `<div>` (`divContent`) below everything else. Click the Insert Div Tag object once more and in the Insert Div Tag dialog, choose divContent for the ID, and After Tag and `<div="divNav">` for the Insert options.

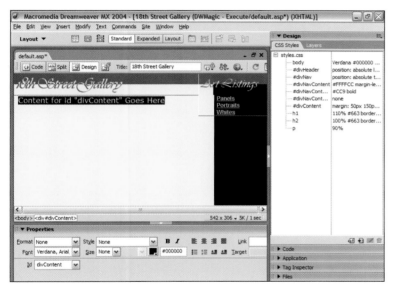

10 Save your work.

Creating the Includes

Now that you have all your pieces in place, you are going to chop it up into separate files to use throughout the site. Every page will use the nav.asp file that you'll create in this section.

1 If it's not still open, open default.asp.

2 Switch to Code view, highlight everything between the `<body>` tag and `<div id="divContent">`, and cut the content to your Clipboard.

3 Open **nav.asp** in the **includes** folder. Highlight everything in the document, and paste the copied code from default.asp.

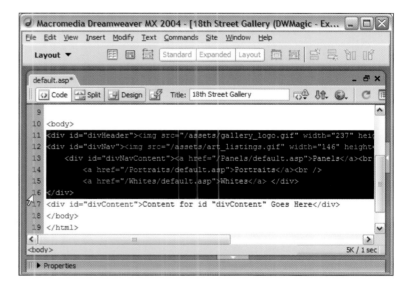

4 Save and close the file. The nav.asp file should now have just the header and navigational `<div>` tags.

5   Return to default.asp, and choose Insert > HTML > Script Objects >
    Server-Side Include to insert the nav.asp include where the original
    navigational elements were, directly below the <body> tag. Your page
    should now look exactly as it did before you set up the nav.asp
    include file.

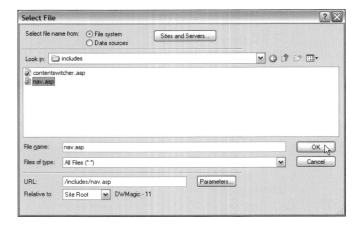

6   In the default.asp page you've been working on, copy the entire page
    in Code view. Open each default.asp file in the gallery subfolders,
    switch to Code view, and paste the copied code. Verify the paths are
    correct for the CSS file and the include.

    You've now made the rest of the default.asp pages match the first one.

7   Save your work.

Powering the Content Switcher with *Server.Execute*

The fun part of this project is finally here! In this section, you're going to
put together all the code for the content switcher. All this will be done
inside contentswitcher.asp inside the includes folder.

1   Open contentswitcher.asp inside the includes folder in your site,
    switch to Code view, and delete everything in the file. You need to
    start with a completely clean slate.

Tip: To save you the trouble of deleting everything in a default ASP
VBScript page, instead create a new text file that is already empty by
default. Just be sure to save the file with an .asp file extension.

---

2   Define the `strCurrentFolder` variable and assign the full page path to
    it by using `Request.ServerVariables("PATH_INFO")`.

    You'll use the `strCurrentFolder` variable to check which folder the
    current page is in so you can display the correct menu to the viewer.
    The variable will contain the full folder path. So if a page is at
    `http://localhost/dir1/dir2/page.asp`, then `PATH_INFO` will return
    `/dir1/dir2/page.asp`.

    Listing 11.1

```
<%
Dim strCurrentPage
strCurrentPage = Request.ServerVariables("PATH_INFO")
```

3   Create an array to define which folders will show which menus. In the
    array, the folders and menus are listed as folder1, menu1, folder2,
    menu2, and so on.

Note: If you want an exact folder match, include the leading and trailing backslashes in your folder names. Use /Panels/ to ensure only files in the Panels folder will be matched. If you use Panels, then files in Panels-Large and Panels-Small will both be matched.

Listing 11.2

```
Dim arMenus
arMenus = Array("/Panels/","panels.asp",
➥"/Portraits/","portraits.asp",
➥"/Whites/","whites.asp")
```

4   Define the strMenuFolder variable and assign it the value /menus/. Be certain to include both the leading and trailing slashes. This variable will define which folder all your menus are stored in. You need to make sure that this path is relative to the site root so that no matter where the page your viewer is looking at is located, the path to the executed menus will be correct.

Listing 11.3

```
Const strMenuFolder = "/menus/"
```

5   Define the variable i to do the counting through your array, and define bolFoundMatch to store whether or not you've actually found a valid match of a folder name in your array. Set the bolFoundMatch variable to False by default.

Listing 11.4

```
Dim i 'Use to loop through our array
Dim bolFoundMatch 'Use to store result of match testing.
bolFoundMatch = False
```

6   Use the next line of code to start looping through the arMenus array two items at a time. You move through the array two at a time to do comparisons on every other entry in the array. The even numbered entries (arrays start at 0, not 1) are the folder names, and the odd numbered entries are the menu filenames. In the next step, you'll do the actual checking.

Listing 11.5

```
For i = 0 To UBound(arMenus) Step 2
```

Note: For/Next loops make it extremely easy to loop through a predefined list of values. This statement says to start at the first element (arrays are 0 based) and go to the upper bound (UBound) of the array, stepping through the array two elements at a time.

7   Use the InStr function to test the strCurrentPage variable, which contains the page path, against the current item in the array.

Listing 11.6

```
If InStr(strCurrentPage,arMenus(i)) > 0 Then
```

To test for a string's value inside another string, the InStr function takes two arguments: the string to search through (strCurrentPage) and the string you want to look for (arMenus(i)). The InStr function returns the position of the first occurrence of the searched for string. If no match is found, InStr returns 0. So if InStr returns a number greater than 0, you've found a match.

8   If you find a match, you need to do a number of things inside the `If` statement: use `Server.Execute` to add the menu to the page, set the `bolFoundMatch` variable to `True`, and exit the `For` loop.

This step is where you'll see the real power of `Server.Execute`. There's absolutely no way those three little lines of code could be accomplished without massive amounts of hand coding using standard includes. The `Server.Execute` method adds the appropriate menu to the page based on the values you created in your array. To add another menu to the site, just add two more entries into the `arMenus` array, and you're set.

Listing 11.7

```
    Server.Execute(strMenuFolder & arMenus(i + 1)
    bolFoundMatch = True
    Exit For
  End If
Next
```

So you can see how it all fits together, here's the entire code block for steps 6 through 8.

Listing 11.8

```
For i = 0 To UBound(arMenus) Step 2
  If InStr(strCurrentPage,arMenus(i)) > 0 Then
    Server.Execute(strMenuFolder & arMenus(i + 1)
    bolFoundMatch = True
    Exit For
  End If
Next
```

9   If the checks find no match, either use `Server.Execute` to pull in a default menu or simply display a message to the viewer.

Listing 11.9

```
If bolFoundMatch = False Then
  Response.Write("No Menu Match Found.")
  'or Server.Execute("/menus/menu.asp")
End If
%>
```

10   Open nav.asp again, and add the contentswitcher.asp include where you want the dynamic data to display. Place the insertion point where you want the content switcher and choose Insert > HTML > Script Objects > Server-Side Include; browse to the contentswitcher.asp file and click OK.

In the finished files provided with the project, the content switcher is added directly below the links to the individual sections in the site.

Listing 11.10

```
<a href="/Whites/Default.asp">Whites</a><br />
<br />
<strong>Gallery Sections</strong><br />
<!--#include virtual="/includes/contentswitcher.asp" -->
```

Now that you've added the content switcher include to the nav.asp include, you're all done, and your menu switcher should show the appropriate content for each main section of your site.

Now Try This

By now you've learned how to design with <div> tags and includes, create the includes, and power the Content Switcher with Server.Execute.

Here are some ideas on how to apply the skills you've learned or use the project you've completed in other ways:

- Now that you can see some of the power of Server.Execute, you could go on to develop your own little mini-applications to drop into your sites. My blog at www.dansshorts.com includes a completely self-contained calendar that is included using Server.Execute, and sidebars added with Server.Execute only when needed (they're gone on the photo gallery pages).

- Using Server.Execute allows you to quickly and easily add and remove parts of your site as necessary, without bogging down server memory or bloating your site's code. The accompanying CD even includes a Server.Execute translator, which allows Dreamweaver to let you view your executed files in Design view, and an object to quickly add new Server.Execute calls.

PROJECT 12

Producing a Sophisticated Interface for CMS with ColdFusion

Angela C.
Buraglia

Massimo Foti

Daniel Short

Angela C. Buraglia is perhaps best known as the founder of Dreamweaver FAQ.com, a site dedicated to serving the Dreamweaver community which she continues to run today with Daniel Short.

Massimo Foti has been a prolific extension developer since the pioneering days of Dreamweaver 1.

Daniel Short is the chief developer for Web Shorts Site Design and a devoted Team Macromedia Volunteer.

Angela C. Buraglia

Massimo Foti

Daniel Short

More and more professional developers are being asked to give their clients more control over their sites. We've been building content management systems for ages, but never really had a way to allow our clients to build sites with valid code. We were always "cleaning up" after them, fixing bad tags or just not letting them enter tags at all.

So to that end, we give you the ColdFusion XHTML Editor. No more messy client code to deal with.

It Works Like This

Our objective is to create a sophisticated, feature-rich interface for a Content Management System (CMS). The cornerstone of this project is the CF XHTML Editor, an online editor that, unlike its competitors, outputs clean and standards-compliant code. The CF XHTML Editor integrates seamlessly inside Dreamweaver's development environment. The whole process is totally automated thanks to extensions; there will be no need to look at any code, much less touch the code directly. Here are the basic steps for the project:

1   Create a table on the Administrator home page to hold the listing of records.

2   Build and test an Insert Record page to test a Content Management System.

3   Create an edit page where you can change and delete records.

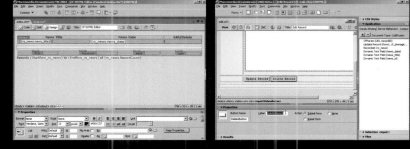

Here, you're creating a table on the Administrator home page and building an Insert Record page.

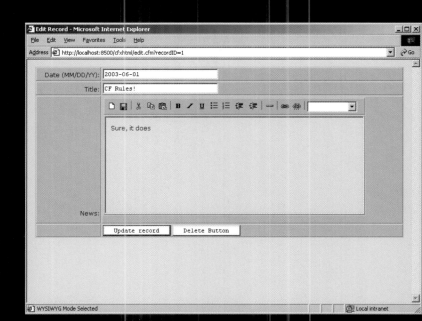

The edit page you will create in this project enables you to change and delete records.

Preparing to Work

To prepare for this project, you will need to do the following:

1   Install two extensions, both by Massimo Foti: **cf_xhtmleditor.mxp** and **confirm_msg.mxp**, found in the **Projects/12/Extensions** folder on the CD. See Appendix A, "Installing Extensions," for more information.

2   Copy the **styles.css** file and the **database** folder from **Projects/12** on the CD to your local machine.

3   Define a new site using the project copy as your site root. Be sure to set up a testing server using the ColdFusion server model.

4   Create a DSN in ColdFusion Administrator called **cf_dwmagic** pointing to **\database\cf_dwmagic.mdb**. See Appendix B, "Creating Database Connections," for more information.

> **Browser Compatibility**
>
> The CF XHTML Editor is designed only for Internet Explorer 6+, making it Windows only. Because it is used in a controlled environment—administrators adding records to a database—it is entirely acceptable that only a single browser is supported.

Setting Up Your Base Pages

To get started, you need a base set of files. You're going to create one default page to start with, and then create copies of that file for the rest of your application. This will ensure that every page is XHTML-compliant and has the proper ColdFusion encoding.

You're obviously aiming for compliant code (why else would you be reading a chapter about an XHTML Editor), so start with an XHTML-compliant document and then attach your CSS file. You'll need to make sure the document has all of the proper ColdFusion encoding as well. Because you'll need four separate files for the administration area and one more file for displaying records to the site's visitors, you'll be doing a bit of File > Save As to speed things up.

1   Create a new XHTML file by choosing File > New, and in the Dynamic Page category, select ColdFusion.

2   Check the Make Document XHTML Compliant box, and click the Create button.

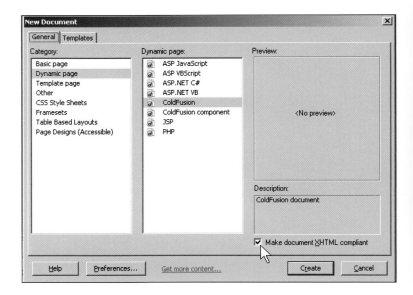

3   Save the document as <u>index.cfm</u> in the root of your defined site.

4   Attach the Cascading Style Sheet. If the CSS Styles panel is not already open, choose Window > CSS Styles to open it.

5   Click the Attach Style Sheets icon in the lower part of the panel.

6   Click the Browse button in the Link External Stylesheet dialog. Locate and select style.css, and click OK.

7   You need to ensure that the document uses the proper encoding for ColdFusion MX Server. If you're using ColdFusion 5, you may skip this part. If you are using ColdFusion MX, choose Insert > ColdFusion Objects > Advanced > CF Page Encoding.

Listing 12.1

```
<cfprocessingdirective pageencoding="iso-8859-1">
<cfcontent type="text/html; charset=iso-8859-1">
<cfset setEncoding("URL", "iso-8859-1")>
<cfset setEncoding("Form", "iso-8859-1")>
```

Note: ColdFusion MX uses utf-8 encoding by default. If you need to deal with ColdFusion MX and localization, www.dwmagic.com/go/7 is a must-read.

8   Save index.cfm to save the page encoding you just added.

9   Save four additional copies: display.cfm, edit.cfm, ie_only.cfm, and insert.cfm. These five files will serve as the base documents for this project.

Note: Be sure to add password protection to admin pages to prevent unauthorized user access. See Dreamweaver's Help section for information on the User Authentication Server behaviors.

The Administrator Home Page

The admin home page is the perfect place to have a hyperlink for adding new records, as well as a listing of existing records that may be edited or deleted. In this section, you'll create a table to hold the listing of records, with appropriate links to the insert.cfm page where you add new records and the edit.cfm page to edit each record.

Creating the Recordset

To begin, you need a page to list all of the records to be edited. First thing you need to do is create a recordset.

1   With index.cfm open, open the Bindings panel in the Application panel group.

Note: If you don't have check marks next to steps 1 through 5 in the Bindings or Server Behaviors panel, you won't be able to create a recordset. See the "Preparing to Build Dynamic Sites" section of Dreamweaver's Help section for more information.

2   Click the (+) icon and choose Recordset (Query).

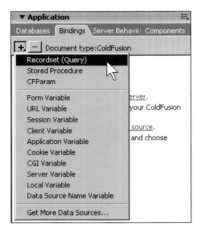

3   Complete the Recordset dialog:

   Name: rs_news

   Data Source: cf_dwmagic

   User Name: leave blank

   Password: leave blank

   Table: News

   Columns: All

   Filter: None

   Sort: news_date and Descending

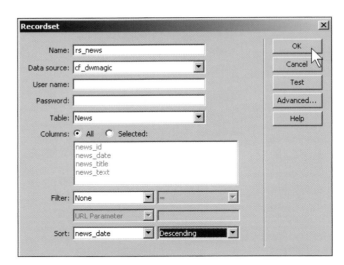

4   Click Test to verify the connection, and click OK after the test has completed successfully.

Building the Master-Detail Page Set

Now that you can get all of the information out of the database, it's time to display it to the user.

1   With index.cfm open, choose Insert > Application Objects > Master Detail Page Set.

Tip: The Master Detail Page Set makes it quick and easy to add a listing page with links directly to a detail page that displays the records from your database.

2   Complete the Master Detail Page Set dialog:

    Recordset: rs_news

    Master Page Fields:

        news_id: Click the (–) button to remove this field from the Master page

        news_date: Press the down arrow to move this below the news_title

        news_text: Remove this field

    Link To Detail From: news_title

    Pass Unique Key: news_id, leave Numeric checked

    Show: 10 Records at a Time

    Detail Page Name: display.cfm

    Detail Page Fields:

        news_id: Remove the news_id. Click the up and down arrows to put the fields into the order you want them to be displayed on the detail page

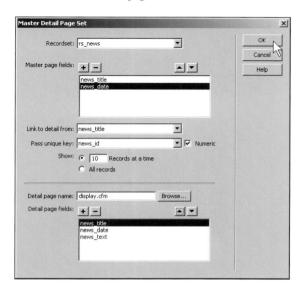

3   Click OK. Now that the Master Detail Page Set has been applied, you should see that display.cfm is now open.

4   Switch to display.cfm (click the document's tab), and save and close the document.

> **Note:** If you're an XHTML code fiend like we are, you may not appreciate the table formatting the default Application Objects add. We suggest you always remove all of the default Dreamweaver-inserted formatting, such as table borders and alignment attributes, both on the table cells and the table itself. Replace them with CSS definitions instead.

5   Switch back to index.cfm. Add another column to the content table to hold the Edit/Delete buttons. Move your mouse above the table until the cursor changes to show a small table grid below the mouse, and click to select the entire table.

6   In the Property inspector, change the columns field to 3 and press Enter to add a new column to the end of the table.

7   Highlight the first row of the table, and in the Properties inspector, check the Header box to convert the `<td>` tags to `<th>` tags. Modify the first two headers to read <u>News Title</u> and <u>News Date</u> in their respective columns, and then label the last column <u>Edit\Delete</u>.

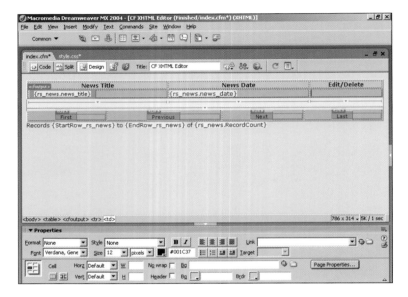

8   Move your mouse over the Title field (which contains {`rs_news.news_title`}) and Ctrl-click/Cmd-click to choose the entire cell. Copy the entire contents of the cell into the Clipboard. Click inside the first table cell under the Edit/Delete header, and paste the contents.

9   Change the hyperlink's text to <u>Edit/Delete</u>. In the Properties inspector, delete `display` from display.cfm and replace it with <u>edit</u> so the link now points to `edit.cfm?recordID=#rs_news.news_id#`.

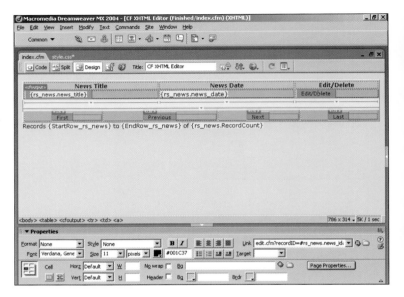

10 Place your cursor somewhere outside of the content table and create a hyperlink pointing to insert.cfm, using <u>Add New Item</u> as the text. Save and close the file. At this point you should be able to preview index.cfm and move back and forth between index.cfm and display.cfm by clicking the news title and the browser's back button.

Inserting New Records

The only real way to test a Content Management System is to manage some content. In this section, you'll build and test an Insert Record page.

1   Open insert.cfm. The page should be blank except for the attached style sheet and the CF Page Encoding.

2   Choose Insert > Application Objects > Insert Record > Record Insertion Form Wizard.

3   Complete the Record Insertion Form dialog, and click OK:

   Data Source: cf_dwmagic

   User Name: blank

   Password: blank

   Table: News

   After Inserting, Go To: <u>index.cfm</u>

   Pass Original Query String: Unchecked

   Form Fields:

   news_id: Remove the field

   news_date: Change the label to <u>Date (MM/DD/YY)</u>: and make sure the submit as column is set to <u>Text</u>

   news_title: Change the label to <u>Title:</u>

   news_text: Change the label to <u>News:</u>

Note: Every database system uses a slightly different way to store dates. Submitting your date information as plain text ensures that you can move your data easily between different database systems with little worry about breaking things.

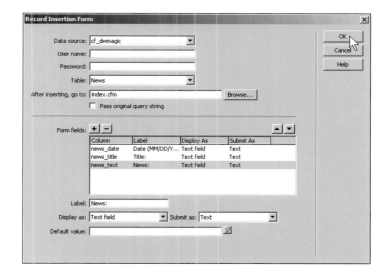

4   Click the news_text form field (the field next to the News: label) in Design view, and press the Delete key to remove the field. As soon as the field is deleted, you should notice that the Insert Record server behavior has a red exclamation point next to it in the Server Behaviors panel. This is Dreamweaver's way of telling you there is something wrong with the page. This will go away as soon as you insert the CF XHTML Editor.

5   With your cursor in the cell where you want to insert the CF XHTML Editor, choose Insert > ColdFusion Objects > Advanced > XHTML Editor.

6   Complete the XHTML Editor dialog, and click OK to add the XHTML Editor to your page.

> Field Name: news_text. The field name should match the name of the field that you deleted.
>
> Field Value: Blank. Because you're inserting a new record, leave this blank.
>
> Redirect: ie_only.cfm. This is the page to which you want to redirect users who don't have IE 6.0.
>
> CSS File: style.css. Because the Editor is actually rendered in an iFrame in insert.cfm, it needs it's own CSS file to use for styling the preview.
>
> Width: Blank. Leave this field blank to make the XHTML Editor size the field for you. The minimum value is 520 pixels.
>
> Height: 300. This measurement is in pixels and will adjust the height of the editing area. The minimum value is 200.

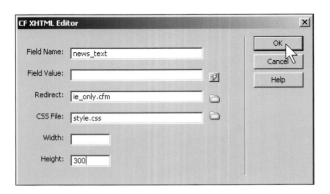

Tip: Because the XHTML Editor has its own CSS file to use for previewing edits, you can use any CSS file you'd like for the preview. It doesn't have to be the same one you're using for your administrative pages.

7   Be sure to upload the CustomTags directory to your testing server before testing your pages.

Inserting the CF XHTML Editor makes several changes to insert.cfm and your site. It inserts the editor and adds an onSubmit behavior to your <form> tag. The Commit XHTML Editor behavior is required in order for changes inside the editor to be added to your database. It also creates a CustomTags directory at the root of your site.

8   Save your work.

Note: Never release an app to your users until you've tested. Open your insert.cfm page in a browser and add a record to test and make sure that everything is working.

Editing and Deleting Records

What happens when you misspell your boss' name or need to get rid of a record that you added last week? In this section, you'll be creating an Edit page where you can change and delete records.

1   Open edit.cfm from the Files panel.

2   Open index.cfm and open the Bindings panel. Select the rs_news recordset, right-click/Ctrl-click, choose Copy, and close index.cfm. In edit.cfm, right-click/Ctrl-click in the Bindings panel and choose Paste.

    To edit a record, you first need to copy over the recordset full of data to retrieve the information on the edit page.

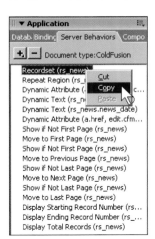

3   Double-click the rs_news recordset in the Bindings panel to open the Recordset dialog. For the Filter drop-down, choose news_id. Leave the next two fields at their defaults, = and URL Parameter. Enter recordID in the last field, which is the URL parameter passed from index.cfm.

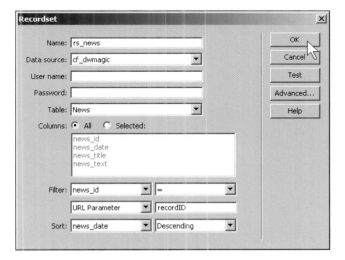

4   Insert an Update Record Form by using Insert > Application Objects > Update Record > Record Update Form Wizard.

5 Complete the Record Update Form dialog:

> Data Source: cf_dwmagic
>
> User Name: blank
>
> Password: blank
>
> Table to Update: News
>
> Select Record From: rs_news
>
> Unique Key Column: news_id, leave Numeric checked
>
> After Updating, Go To: index.cfm
>
> Pass Original Querystring: Unchecked
>
> Form Fields:
>
>> news_id: Remove the record ID. The user should never be allowed to change IDs.
>>
>> news_date: Change the label to Date (MM/DD/YY): and ensure the date is submitted as Text
>>
>> news_title: Change the label to Title:
>>
>> news_text: Change the label to News:

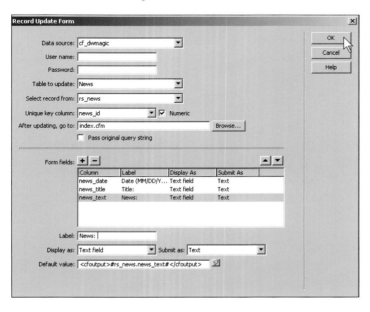

6 Click the news_date text field, open the Bindings panel, open the List menu in the format column for the news_date, and choose Date/Time > 01/17/00. This sets the date to an easily readable format.

Tip: You can add the Validate Form behavior to ensure the date is in the desired format before submitting the form.

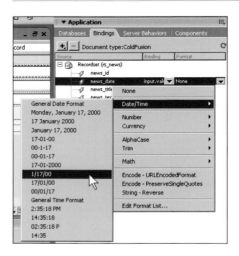

7 Click the text field for News and press Delete to remove it. Leave the cursor in the table cell and choose Insert > ColdFusion Objects > Advanced > XHTML Editor and complete the CF XHTML Editor dialog and click OK.

> Field Name: news_text
>
> Field Value: Click the lightning bolt icon, choose news_text from the rs_news recordset, click OK
>
> Redirect: ie_only.cfm
>
> CSSfile: style.css
>
> Width: blank
>
> Height: 300

Similar to what you did for the insert, this removes the default field for news_text and replaces it with the editor.

8 Save edit.cfm to test editing records.

Note: Again, be sure to test your edit page by clicking a record on your index.cfm page and completing the form on edit.cfm.

Now that you have editing working, it's time to add a button to delete records.

1 Continuing in edit.cfm, place your cursor next to the Update Record button and add a new form button by choosing Insert > Form > Button.

2 Name the button DeleteButton and change the label to Delete Record.

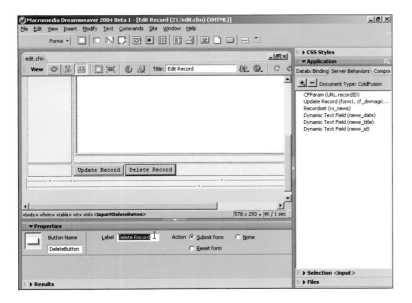

3 To add the server behavior, choose Insert > Application Objects > Delete Record or click the Delete Record object from the Application category of the Insert bar.

4 Complete the Delete Record dialog, and click OK.

First Check If Variable Defined: Choose Form Variable from the drop-down list, enter DeleteButton in the text field.

Data Source: cf_dwmagic

Username: blank

Password: blank

Table: News

Primary Key Column: news_id, leave Numeric checked

Primary Key Value: Choose Form Variable from the drop-down, and leave the text field news_id.

After Deleting, Go To: index.cfm

The Primary Key Value setting will pull the current record's ID from a hidden form field in the page.

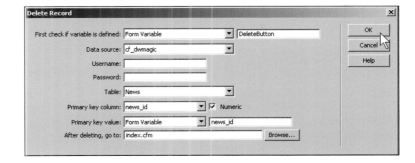

5 Select the Delete Record button in Design view. Open the Behaviors panel. Click the (+) button and choose Massimocorner > Confirm Message. Complete the Confirm Message dialog, and click OK.

Because your Update and Delete buttons are so close together, you should make sure that the user really wants to delete the selected record. Adding the Confirm Message behavior to the Delete button onClick fixes this.

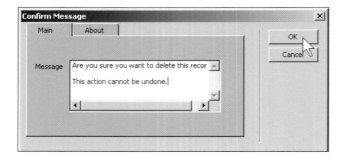

Tip: We like to make our Delete buttons a different color by using some CSS styling. Make it as obvious as possible to the user that your Delete button can do some damage.

6 Switch to Code view, and click the Delete Record server behavior in the Server Behaviors panel to highlight the delete code. Cut the selected code using Edit > Cut.

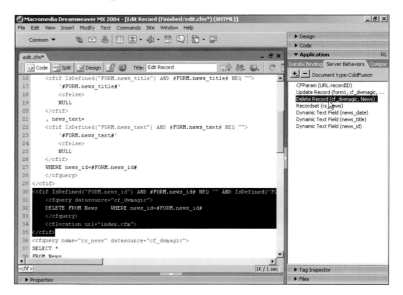

Because you used Record Update Form Wizard first, the Delete Record server behavior is inserted after the update. This means that when you click Delete Record, the record would be updated in the database, and then deleted. This isn't an efficient way to handle things, so you need to move the code manually in Code view to improve it.

7 Click the Update Record server behavior in the Server Behaviors panel to select the Update Record block of code in Code view. Place your cursor before the Update Record code block on line 7, and paste in the delete code using Edit > Paste. Choose View > Refresh Design View, or press F5 to update the Server Behaviors panel.

You should now see the Delete Record server behavior above the Update Record server behavior.

Tip: To avoid needing to touch the code manually to move server behaviors around, simply build your form manually and apply the server behaviors in the order you want them to happen.

Note: Check to make sure the Delete button is working properly by testing the Delete Record button on your edit page.

Now Try This

By now you've learned how to create a table on the Administrator home page to hold the listing of records, build and test an Insert Record page to test a Content Management System, and create an edit page where you can change and delete records.

Here are some ideas on how to apply the skills you've learned or use the project you've completed in other ways:

- You're not limited to just one XHTML Editor on a page. If you have several fields that require user input, then you can place as many XHTML editors on your page as you wish.

- As far as other modifications go, this application really stands on its own. To get the most out of the XHTML Editor, you need to add pieces around it to make data insertion easier. Consider using the Date Picker used in Project 7, "Using Flash in Dreamweaver," for making date insertion easier for your users.

APPENDIX A | Installing Extensions

This appendix provides instructions on how to install the extensions found on the book's accompanying CD-ROM.

1   Launch the Extension Manager.

The Extension Manager can be launched by choosing Commands > Manage Extensions.

2   Verify that Dreamweaver MX 2004 is chosen in the list menu.

3   Choose File > Install Extension.

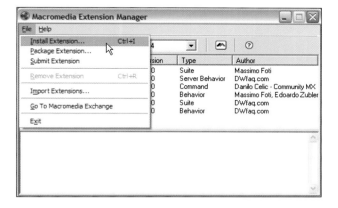

4   Browse to the extension's folder on the CD.

If a project has an extension, you'll find it located in **Projects\ ##\Extensions** where ## is the number of the project.

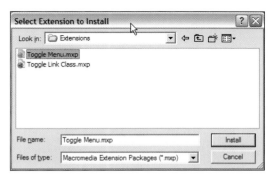

5   Accept the license agreement and the installation confirmation. You may be prompted to restart Dreamweaver.

6   In the top portion of the Extension Manager, select the extension you just installed by clicking on the name.

7   Carefully read the description and access information in the bottom portion of the Extension Manager.

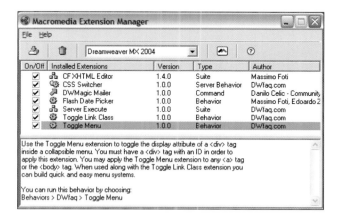

Creating Database Connections

This appendix will cover creating database connections in Dreamweaver MX 2004. To create a dynamic page in Dreamweaver, you need to create a connection to your Data Source. There are several different combinations of databases and drivers that you can use for each server model, but they all work about the same way. This appendix looks at how to set up common connections for the most popular databases in Dreamweaver. If you are using a different driver or database, the process should be roughly the same, but the dialogs or wording may be slightly different.

Creating ColdFusion Data Sources

Adding new Data Sources in ColdFusion is simple. If you're testing on a remote server and don't have access to the ColdFusion administrator, contact your host and have them set up the Data Source for you. If you're testing locally, open the ColdFusion Administrator from the Start menu.

1 Log in using the password you supplied when you installed ColdFusion.

2 Click Data Sources under Data & Services on the left side.

3 On the Data Sources page enter a name for your Data Source Name, cf_dwmagic for example.

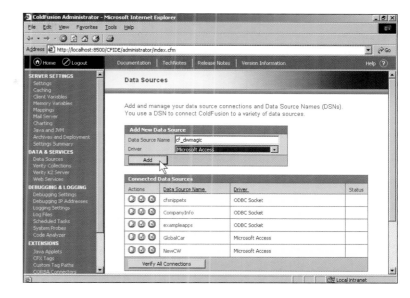

4 In the Driver drop-down menu, choose Microsoft Access.

5 Click Add.

6   On the Microsoft Access Data Source page, click Browse Server next to Database File and browse to your local database. Highlight the mdb file, and click Apply.

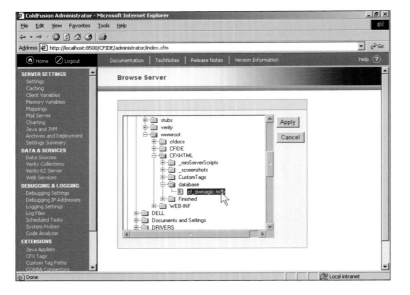

7   Back on the Microsoft Access Data Source page, click Submit.

You should be returned to the Data Sources page with the message "datasource updated successfully." If you receive any errors, check the Macromedia Support site (www.dwmagic.com/go/5) for more information. For additional information on working with ColdFusion Data Sources, see www.dwmagic.com/go/4.

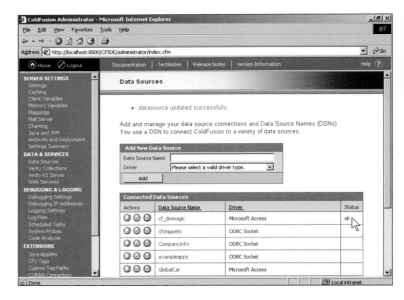

Creating ASP.NET Database Connections

1   With an ASP.NET document open, go to the Application panel and click on the Databases tab. Click the plus (+) sign, and select OLE DB Connection.

This adds a new Dreamweaver database connection. In this book, a Microsoft Access database is used because of its sheer ease of use. Keep in mind that although an Access database is good for a small-scale site, its effectiveness declines as traffic grows.

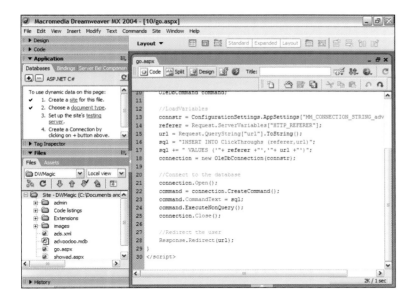

2   In the OLE DB Connection dialog box, give the connection a name—in this case, <u>advoodoo</u>.

3   Click the Build button to bring up the Data Link Properties dialog.

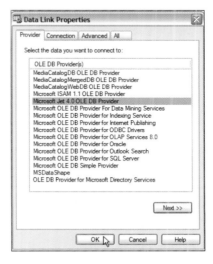

4   In the Data Link Properties' Provider tab, choose Microsoft Jet 4.0 OLE DB Provider and click Next.

5   Browse to the location of your access database in the Connection tab. Test the connection to ensure everything is correct, and click OK to close out the Data Link Properties dialog.

6   Click OK to close out the OLE DB Connection dialog.

Behind the scenes, Dreamweaver creates an entry in your web.config file, or if you don't have a web.config file, Dreamweaver will create it with an appropriate entry for your database connection.

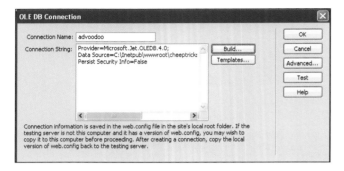

Creating PHP MySQL Database Connections

Creating connections to a MySQL database with PHP in Dreamweaver is very simple.

1   With a PHP document open, go to the Application panel and click on the Databases tab. Click the plus (+) sign and select the MySQL Connection.

2   In the MySQL Connection dialog, enter a name for your connection, in this case <u>advoodoo</u>.

The name is only for your benefit in the Dreamweaver UI, so name it something descriptive that is going to help you as you create PHP MySQL pages.

3   Set the MySQL Server field to the IP address of your MySQL server. If you are running PHP and MySQL on your machine, then you can enter <u>127.0.0.1</u>.

4   Enter the User Name and the Password for the database.

5   Click on the Select button, select the database that you want to use, and click OK.

6   Test your connection from the MySQL Connection dialog box. Once it tests out correctly, click OK to create the connection.

INDEX

www.informit.com

Voices that Matter™

VIEW CART search
▸ Registration already a member? Log in. ▸ Book Registration

OUR AUTHORS

PRESS ROOM

| :::: web development | :::: design | :::: photoshop | :::: new media | :::: 3-D | :::: server technologies |

EDUCATORS

ABOUT US

CONTACT US

You already know that New Riders brings you the **Voices that Matter**. But what does that mean? It means that New Riders brings you the Voices that challenge your assumptions, take your talents to the next level, or simply help you better understand the complex technical world we're all navigating.

Visit **www.newriders.com** to find:

- ▸ *Discounts* on specific book purchases
- ▸ Never before published chapters
- ▸ Sample chapters and excerpts
- ▸ Author bios and interviews
- ▸ Contests and enter-to-wins
- ▸ Up-to-date industry event information
- ▸ Book reviews
- ▸ Special offers from our friends and partners
  Info on how to join our User Group program
- ▸ Ways to have your Voice heard

New Riders

WWW.NEWRIDERS.COM

VOICES THAT MATTER

VISIT OUR WEB SITE

WWW.NEWRIDERS.COM

On our web site, you'll find information about our other books, authors, tables of contents, and book errata. You will also find information about book registration and how to purchase our books, both domestically and internationally.

EMAIL US

Contact us at: **nrfeedback@newriders.com**

- If you have comments or questions about this book
- To report errors that you have found in this book
- If you have a book proposal to submit or are interested in writing for New Riders
- If you are an expert in a computer topic or technology and are interested in being a technical editor who reviews manuscripts for technical accuracy

Contact us at: **nreducation@newriders.com**

- If you are an instructor from an educational institution who wants to preview New Riders books for classroom use. Email should include your name, title, school, department, address, phone number, office days/hours, text in use, and enrollment, along with your request for desk/examination copies and/or additional information.

Contact us at: **nrmedia@newriders.com**

- If you are a member of the media who is interested in reviewing copies of New Riders books. Send your name, mailing address, and email address, along with the name of the publication or web site you work for.

BULK PURCHASES/CORPORATE SALES

The publisher offers discounts on this book when ordered in quantity for bulk purchases and special sales. For sales within the U.S., please contact: Corporate and Government Sales (800) 382-3419 or **corpsales@pearsontechgroup.com**. Outside of the U.S., please contact: International Sales (317) 428-3341 or **international@pearsontechgroup.com**.

WRITE TO US

New Riders Publishing
800 East 96th Street, 3rd Floor
Indianapolis, IN 46240

CALL/FAX US

Toll-free (800) 571-5840
If outside U.S. (317) 428-3000
Ask for New Riders
FAX: (317) 428-3280

New Riders